THE
PLANT BUYER'S
DIRECTORY

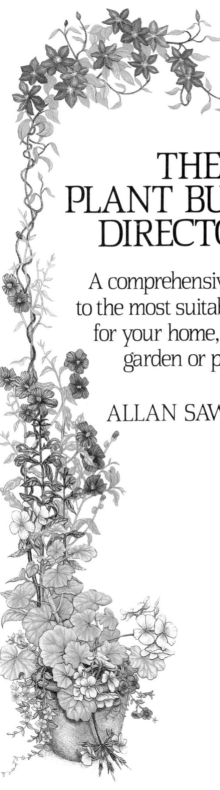

THE PLANT BUYER'S DIRECTORY

A comprehensive guide
to the most suitable plants
for your home, terrace,
garden or patio

ALLAN SAWYER

EBURY PRESS
LONDON

Published by Ebury Press
Division of The National Magazine Company Ltd
Colquhoun House
27-37 Broadwick Street
London W1V 1FR

First impression 1986

ISBN 0 85223 428 7

Designed and produced by Robert Adkinson Limited, London.

Editorial Director
Clare Howell

Art Director
Christine Simmonds

Editor
Janet Law

Designer
Mike Rose

Illustrations
Julie Stiles

Phototypeset by Ashwell Print Services, Shotesham

Colour origination by La Cromolito, Milan

Printed and bound in Belgium by Brepols, Turnhout

The author and publishers gratefully acknowledge the assistance of
Dr Alan Leslie in providing information on plant classification.

Key to symbols

🌺 Flowering period according to months of the year

◯ Full sun   💧 Dry

◐ Semi—shade   💧💧 Average

⬤ Full shade   💧💧💧 Damp

CONTENTS

INTRODUCTION

The range of plants to be found in a garden centre or nursery catalogue is often very large and somewhat bewildering, with little indication as to which are the best cultivars. The aim of this book is to select and illustrate a good basic range of plants, giving all the essential information about each one in a readily accessible form.

The book is divided into the four seasons: Winter (December, January, February); Spring (March, April, May); Summer (June, July, August); and Autumn (September, October, November). The divisions do not, of course, work quite so precisely as this, for plants will flower earlier or later according to their geographical position and the weather in a particular year. A selection of plants from each period will establish a basic framework for the garden, but you will probably discover that your garden naturally divides itself into different areas: winter-flowering shrubs and plants prefer moist, shaded spots and spring bulbs flourish in open spaces, while summer-flowering plants offer sufficient variety for them to be distributed evenly. By taking advantage of this you can concentrate your efforts on one part of the garden at a time, allowing the focus to move as the year progresses.

Within this framework you can create more variety by planting annuals and bedding schemes, incorporating tender plants such as fuchsias and begonias which have over-wintered in the greenhouse. Alternatively, you may prefer to complete a design with permanent planting and then leave it alone.

The list of suggested plants is by no means exhaustive, and it may be that particular plants thrive in your garden and you are encouraged to acquire a collection of their kindred. You might, for instance, be fortunate in having a moist, acid soil in which rhododendrons and camellias flourish, so you could begin to collect more of these beautiful spring-flowering shrubs.

All the recommendations in this book are currently available commercially and most should be stocked in any good garden centre. Failing that, they could be ordered from the garden centre or from one of the specialist nurseries whose catalogues make such tempting reading on a wet Sunday afternoon.

Allan Sawyer

PLANT SELECTION

It is essential when selecting plants to consider the basic nature of your garden, its design, type of soil and requirements in terms of shade and privacy. If you rush out to a garden centre and select plants on the basis of how much you like them as individuals, you may find that, like guests at a party, they fail to get on with each other. You cannot plant sun-loving plants near a fast-growing hedge which will cast a long, dense shadow after a few years, shrubs near the edge of a path, or large trees in positions where they will eventually become a nuisance and have to be felled.

Garden design

Garden design is a large and challenging subject which is really outside the scope of this book, but it is necessary to establish a good 'skeleton' to your garden before considering your planting schemes. A good design can create enormous interest, and even an illusion of space, in the smallest garden. No amount of lovely plants, on the other hand, can transform a poorly thought-out plot into a satisfactory garden.

With the actual layout, certain fundamental points are worth bearing in mind. A small garden subdivided into two or three sections will look much larger than the same garden with a single open space in the centre and planting around the perimeter. Circles and diagonal lines have the effect of making a narrow garden appear wider, and the planting of brightly coloured flowering plants close to the house and soft pastel shades further away creates an impression of depth in a short garden.

You may be planning a garden from scratch or taking over an established one, with mature trees, shrubs and landscape features. In either case, it is worth devoting some attention to the design, if necessary referring to books for inspiration. Do not be disheartened by the size of your garden. New gardeners often find themselves surprised by the discovery that the more they put in a garden they larger it seems. Tiny city gardens seem to expand enormously once their walls or fences are clothed in climbing plants and one or two carefully positioned trees established. Even in a purely ornamental garden there is a place for a small area to grow herbs and salad vegetables, or apples on dwarfing rootstock which make delightful trees, making it productive as well as pretty.

Once the basic design of the garden has been

PLANT SELECTION

decided, you can turn your attention to the plants. These, too, will do much to 'shape' the garden, especially if they are chosen for their form and foliage, rather than simply for their flowers, which may be fairly short-lived. Some plants, especially trees and the larger shrubs, can be used singly to create focus points, but generally speaking herbaceous plants and small shrubs are best planted in groups of three or five to create a bold effect. A border or bed with just one of everything can look messy and create unnecessary work. If, though, you are uncertain as to how well a particular plant will look in your garden, or whether it will be happy in your soil, then it is wise to buy one plant initially and then to propagate it or buy more the following season.

A garden that is planted for a single effect such as a riot of daffodils and tulips in spring or a blaze of summer glory in June and July, is disappointing for the rest of the year, so it is advisable to have a number of key plants which are interesting and attractive at different periods. Even in winter there are plants with ornamental berries or flowers, which planted near the house, will gladden the cold, dark days.

Basic plants which are to form the main features of a garden should be selected and planted first. Conifers, evergreen shrubs and specimen trees must be positioned with an eye to their eventual size and the way in which they will alter the focus and shape of the garden as they develop. A fast-growing conifer hedge must be stopped at the right height (usually 2 to 2.5m/6½ to 8ft), for if it is allowed to grow too tall and then cut back it will look ugly; a wide spreading tree should be positioned so that the shade cast in later years is not seriously detrimental to the plants growing around it; rapid-growing ground-cover plants must be kept within bounds and not permitted to smother less vigorous plants or over-run paths and paved areas. 'Architectural' perennials and shrubs grown for their foliage and striking seasonal displays should be planted where they can be seen from two or three sides.

In planting flower-beds and borders you should take due account of the eventual size of the plants, placing the tall ones at the back and smaller ones in front. There is no reason, however, to be too dogmatic about this. A tall, relatively slim plant, such as aconitum or kniphoffia, can be positioned near the front of a border to break up the line and draw the eye down a path; similarly, a slight hollow created by a low-growing plant in the centre of a border can sometimes allow one to appreciate more fully the tall specimens such as phlox or delphiniums growing at the back. The visual effect of these plants will become obvious within three or four seasons and if they are not satisfactory they can be moved or given away. The more substantial plants should be given plenty of space to develop properly. Rather than placing them too close together for an 'instant' effect, it is better to fill the gaps with annuals for a few years.

One particularly rewarding feature of a well-planned garden is the association of different plants, and by using your imagination, you can create many delightful surprises at each time of year. The bluish-white flowers of *Scilla campanulata* will complement the pale green of *Helleborus corsicus* in the spring, roses mingle happily with clematis in the summer and bright-pink nerines with the vivid red hips of *Rosa moyesii* provide flashes of colour among the muted tones of autumn.

Soil and aspect

Certain plants, such as camellias or clematis, only perform well in an acid or alkaline soil, so if you wish to grow these it is advisable to test your soil with one of the simple kits available from most garden centres and shops. Alternatively, you can see what is growing in the neighbourhood, but this is not always a conclusive indicator for the soil may vary from street to street. Plants can, of course, be grown in an unsympathetic soil area, but only if they are provided with a generous supply of the right acid or alkaline soil in their hole or tub.

Attention must be given to the nature of the site into which the plant is going. If you are intending to plant subjects that like a dry, well-drained soil and your garden is low-lying and wet, then you can accommodate them by raising the level of the beds with low brick walls, old railway sleepers or a wall of peat blocks. Trailing plants, such as arabis, iberis, aubrieta and gentian, will soon disguise the wall and the difference will be quite sufficient to allow crocus, thyme, daffodils, cistus, nerines and similar damp-hating plants to survive. On the other hand, the soil may be open and free-draining. If then, you wish to plant moisture-loving subjects, you should incorporate plenty of leafmould and compost into the soil, or line the bottom and sides of a large hole (1m by 2m/3ft by 6½ft) with old polythene fertilizer bags or a piece of butyl pond-liner to create a small damp area for astilbes, zantedeschias, dwarf rhododendrons, spirea, phlox and other thirsty subjects. These methods only work, of course, with herbaceous plants and small or medium-sized shrubs.

The amount of sun a plant receives is often crucial to its general health and its ability to produce flowers. Sometimes perennials and shrubs suited to light or semi-shade will still thrive in complete shade, but they will grow somewhat smaller in stature and spread. This may even be an advantage, for rampant plants such as the plume-poppy *Macleaya* or polygonums are less likely to strangle their neighbours.

Buying plants

Plants may be bought either through a mail-order catalogue or at a nursery or garden centre. In either case, you should reassure yourself that they are of good quality and have been grown with care. When buying through the post you are obviously at the mercy of the supplier, which is all the more reason to select a reputable one; but if you go to a garden centre you can examine the plants yourself. This should be done gently, lifting the plant by its container and never by the stem or lower branches. If there are a mass of roots coming out of the bottom of the container then the plant has probably been in it for too long, but if just one or two are beginning to find their way out, then the plant is ready to be repotted or go into the ground and will establish itself quickly.

Always choose plants with clean, healthy foliage and select small, sturdy, compact ones in preference to leggy, floppy, etiolated specimens. With trees and shrubs in particular, it is true that a small, healthy specimen will establish itself far more easily once it is planted out. Larger plants will have a greater problem in settling in, since their root system is often severely out of proportion to their foliage area. You could find that the 'instant' effect actually deteriorates into slow death, especially if the summer after planting is a long, dry one.

Fortunately, it is not always necessary to buy plants. If you weed carefully in permanently planted beds you will find that many plants throw off numerous seedlings, which can either be exchanged with friends or used to increase your stock.

PLANTING OUT

Plants may be supplied either bare-rooted, that is to say lifted from open ground, or container-grown. In both cases it is worth planting them carefully to achieve the best results.

Bare-rooted plants do not have to be planted immediately, but especially roses and fruit trees will survive for some weeks before being planted, provided that they are protected from frost and their roots kept moist. They should be heeled into a trench and protected with sacking, or stored in a dry frost-free shed with the roots covered by damp sacking or moist peat. Many specialist nurseries will supply plants bare-rooted, dug up in autumn as soon as they are dormant and despatched direct to the customer; if they arrive when the soil is unworkable due to hard frosts or waterlogging, then you have little option but to store them temporarily until conditions are suitable for planting out.

Container-grown plants can be purchased and planted at any time of the year, although it is clearly not beneficial to plant anything during a period of severe frost. They should be given a good soaking before planting, preferably by standing in a bucket for an hour.

The planting hole should be about twice as wide as the root ball and the bottom of the hole should be well dug over, with the addition of a liberal helping of well-rotted compost or leafmould to encourage root development. A handful of bonemeal is a helpful conditioner for undernourished soils. In the case of bare-rooted plants the bottom of the hole should be mounded up towards the centre to allow the roots to be trained outwards and downwards. With container plants the rootball should be disturbed as little as possible except to tease out any roots which have become tangled around the inside of the pot or bag.

After placing the plant in the hole, the rest of the soil should be moved back into position and firmed down either with your hands or, with larger plants, with a heavy boot — but take care not to over compact the soil or root development will be inhibited. Make sure that the plant is set at the right level, either that of the container, or with bare-rooted plants, at the level of its original soil, which can be seen in a ring around the base of the plant.

Standard roses and trees will need the support of a stake, which must be set firmly in position before the planting hole is filled in. This will prevent the wind from loosening the plant and blowing it over. In most cases the stake can be removed after two or three years but with standard roses and similar large-headed, slim-stemmed plants the stakes should really be left in permanently.

Sometimes you will be moving established plants from elsewhere in your garden, rather than installing new ones. The same planting procedure should be followed but as much of the original rootball and soil should be preserved as possible. If you move plants in autumn then you must make sure they do not get lifted by the frost or loosened by wind; with spring plantings you should give the plant an adequate supply of water until the root system has re-established itself.

A bare-rooted plant protected by a bag.

The roots should be arranged over a mound of earth, and if necessary, a stake should be inserted to support the plant.

The earth should be firmed down around the plant and the stake tied securely.

A container-grown plant should be soaked in water before planting.

The roots should be disturbed as little as possible.

Ensure that the plant is set at the right level, with the top of the container-soil level with the surface of the ground.

Proper care of your plants once they are in position will ensure a long and healthy life for them and help maintain a neat appearance in your garden. Herbaceous plants should be cut down to within 10cm (4in) of the ground as soon as the first frosts are over. The small amount of stalk and foliage remaining will protect the crown from frost and act as a marker to prevent the plant from being inadvertently dug up. Modern hybrid roses can be cut back by about one-third in November to a convenient leaf joint and then pruned back again in spring to an outward-facing bud close to the base of the main steam. Plants such as buddleia which flower on their new wood should be pruned in February, just cutting back to the last bud on last year's growth. Evergreen shrubs such as eleagnus and eucalyptus can be thinned and pruned in November and December. Lightly turning the soil between the plants with a hoe or border fork will allow the frost to break up the earth and kill off some of the pests and soil-borne fungal diseases which overwinter in such places, and the removal of leaf-litter and similar waste will discourage slugs, earwigs, woodlice and similar pests.

Pests and diseases

These become a problem for most gardeners sooner or later but if tackled promptly can easily be kept under control or eliminated.

Aphids Greenfly, blackfly, whitefly and woolly aphis usually attack young soft growth and damage the plant by sucking sap. They can spread virus disease and may attract colonies of ants, which feed on the honeydew they produce. Since they are all sap-sucking insects the most efficient way of dealing with them is by the use of a systemic insecticide. This is usually applied by spraying and the chemical is taken into the plant's system to kill off the insects as they feed. The protection remains in the plant for anything up to two weeks and it therefore not only gets rid of the existing infestation but also kills off any new aphids that hatch out. By spraying regularly from the time that the leafbuds open in April until the late summer, you can ensure that your plants never suffer from a build-up of insect pests. If the spraying is done in the evening just before sunset, then beneficial insects such as bees and butterflies are not harmed.

Powdery mildew and blackspot Fungal diseases of this kind can also be treated systemically. Fungicides absorbed into the plant's system will give continuous protection over long periods, but the spraying programme must commence before any signs of infection appear.

Slugs and snails These ground-based pests eat the soft new growth of herbaceous plants and annuals that emerge in the spring. They can be dealt with in two ways. Firstly, with slug pellets or liquid slug killers, which can be watered in around plants which need protection. The liquid killer will also kill off eggs which are just below the surface of the soil, but it will leach away fairly quickly in rainy weather, so it is often necessary to renew the treatment every fortnight. The alternative method of control is to set slug traps which are available from most garden centres. They consist of small dishes filled with beer, which attracts slugs and snails from the surrounding area so they crawl into the trap and drown. The traps must be emptied every other day, but usually after a week or so, you will find that all the slugs and snails within the area of the trap have been eliminated. By using traps in March and April the plants can become well established, and by the time the slug population builds up again they are no longer vulnerable to attack.

Weeding

This can be done by hand, but some weeds, such as bindweed and oxalis, are best treated with chemicals. If you try to dig them up, you simply get new plants growing from the pieces of root left in the soil. However, if you coat the leaves of the plants with a translocated herbicide, such as Tumbleweed, then the weedkiller is absorbed and drawn right down to the roots, eventually killing the entire plant. This method of control is also ideal for eliminating the odd weed which comes up between valued plants and cannot be dug out without endangering its neighbours. Paraquat-based weedkillers, which kill off any seedlings as soon as they germinate, will maintain a clean area around newly planted trees and shrubs; but a layer of bark chippings or grass clippings, 2 or 3cm (about 1⅛ in) thick will effectively smother any seedlings and also act as a moisture-retaining blanket during dry spells. Persistent perennial weeds such as ground elder, dock, nettles and brambles will require stronger treatment, but regular application of chemicals will eventually eliminate them.

WINTER

The idea that there is nothing worth looking at in the garden during winter is clearly a mistaken one. If your main interest is flowers, then there are any number of winter-flowering shrubs, herbaceous plants and bulbs to delight the eye. Usually their impact is in a lower key than that of the spring and summer displays but, after all, they don't have so much competition, and many winter-flowering plants are also sweetly scented which gives them an added attraction on a clear, still, sunny morning. Apart from flowering plants there are, of course, those with ornamental evergreen foliage or coloured bark. These features go largely unnoticed for most of the year but without the distraction of brightly-coloured flowers you are suddenly able to focus on the beautiful shapes formed from the wide range of greens, yellows and blues of broad-leafed and coniferous evergreens, or the fascinating patterns of reds, browns and greens made by the bark of deciduous shrubs such as dogwoods or acers. The greatest pleasure in pottering around in the garden at this time of the year is that all you need to do is look; the autumn pruning and mulching has been done and the spring planting and preparation is yet to come. The lawn has stopped growing and so have the weeds; so, apart from tying back a wind-damaged shrub or pruning out broken shoots or branches, there is really very little to do except observe, enjoy and maybe plan a change or two while you can see the structure of the garden clearly.

WINTER

Abies koreana

Every garden has a spot for a small conifer. The green, blue or golden foliage provides a focus in winter months when many other plants are leafless or have disappeared altogether. The **Korean Fir** has a neat, compact habit and is fairly slow growing. Even after ten years it is unlikely to be more than 2m (6½ft) tall. A striking feature is the blue, barrel-shaped cones. Unlike some other species, the plant begins to bear cones when still quite young. Care must be taken to ensure a plentiful supply of water for the whole of the first season after planting. A good measure of well-soaked peat worked into the ground before planting will help a lot.

A. koreana

○ ▲▲▲

Acer griseum

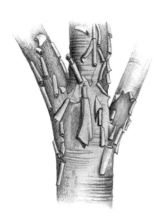

The **Paperbark Maple** is a delightful, small specimen tree ultimately reaching about 12m (40ft) tall. Its elegant foliage turns brilliant scarlet, red and orange in autumn but it should be particularly prized for its fascinating winter appearance when sections of the old bark flake and peel back to reveal a pattern of cinnamon-coloured new bark beneath. It is tolerant of most soils but likes plenty of moisture. Careful attention in its early years to ensure a strong, vertical leading shoot, and the judicious removal of the lowest side branches and any crossing or badly placed shoots, will result in a graceful tree that makes a strong contribution to the design and appearance of your garden.

○ ▲▲

A. griseum

WINTER

Adonis amurensis

A.amurensis

In late winter and early spring the bright, buttercup-yellow flowers of the delightful ground-hugging **Adonis** illuminate many a bare patch on a rockery or at the front of a border. The flowers usually open before the soft green, feathery foliage is fully developed and there are single as well as double flowered forms available. It is quite happy in sun or partial shade but its position should be carefully marked because the whole plant disappears completely in late summer and re-emerges only in January. Each plant attains a height of about 15cm (6in) and a spread of about 10cm (4in).

🌺 2–3 ◑ ●●

Anemone blanda

'Atrocoerulea'

In any open, sunny, well-drained spot, a bold grouping of the **Grecian Windflower** lends a brisk freshness to February mornings. If purchased as tubers, it is a good idea to soak them for twenty-four hours before planting. Set the tubers about 5cm (2in) deep and 5cm apart. The most common form has blue flowers, but named, coloured cultivars — such as 'Radar' with its vivid red flowers and white centre; 'Bridesmaid', a very free flowering white form; or 'Charmer' with deep rosy red flowers — are obtainable. Once established they will spread by scattering their own seed and within a few seasons you will have an attractive spreading mat of colour and fern-like, ground-hugging foliage every year.

🌺 2 ○ ●●

WINTER

Arbutus unedo

'Rubra'

The Killarney **Strawberry Tree** is a handsome and highly ornamental evergreen which produces white or pink flowers and bright red, strawberry-like fruits in November and December. It is lime-tolerant and able to withstand very high winds. The fruits, which take twelve months to ripen, are edible and therefore no danger to children. There are a number of forms of this particular species. 'Integerrima' makes a many-branched shrub rather than a tree and is somewhat shy of flowering. 'Rubra' makes a very choice tree, ultimately attaining about 15m (50ft) in height and producing abundant flowers richly flushed with pink and a bravura display of fruit.

🌺 11–12 ◐ ◆◆

Chamaecyparis obtusa 'Nana Gracilis'

'Nana Gracilis'

An enormously long name for a dainty little conifer. This very slow-growing **Cypress** will eventually make an attractive dark green dome-shaped shrub, but even after ten years it will still be about only 100cm (3¼ ft) high. The fan-shaped foliage in beautifully arranged layers gives the plant a sculpted look making it suitable for a feature in a patio or terrace. Care should be taken to ensure plenty of moisture at the root, especially during the first season after planting, but no feeding is necessary apart from a generous spadeful of compost mixed into the soil before planting. Golden and variegated forms are also offered.

○ ◆◆

WINTER

Chimonanthus praecox

'Luteus'

The **Winter Sweet**, sometimes offered as *C.fragrans*, grows best against a sunny wall. It thrives on well-drained, chalky soils but is fairly happy anywhere except on heavy clay. It takes a few years to settle down and then will surprise you one winter morning with a flush of waxy, sweetly scented, pale yellow flowers on long bare branches. Once the shrub has reached flowering size the long growths can be pruned back each year as the blossoms fade, keeping the shrub to about 2m (6½ft) high by 2m wide. The form 'Luteus' has larger, better-coloured flowers but is less fragrant; 'Grandiflorus' has deep yellow flowers with a prominent red mark at the centre but is seldom offered now.

 2 ○

Clematis cirrhosa balearica

C.cirrhosa balearica

The **Fern Leafed Clematis** will ramble happily up trellises, through shrubs, over trees or anywhere else you put it, provided it finds plenty of 'handholds'. It thrives best in moist but well-drained soils and appreciates a spring dressing of general purpose fertilizer. Being evergreen it is at risk of wind damage in winter in exposed situations. The pale yellow, bell-shaped flowers appear all winter through and are followed by delightful, silky seedheads. Prune in spring, but only to remove dead wood or to take off those shoots which threaten to strangle adjacent plants. You may sometimes find this plant offered as *C.calcina*.

 11–3 ◑

WINTER

Crocus ancyrensis

C.ancyrensis

Golden Bunch is one of the earliest crocuses to flower. On sunny January days the blooms open wide like a chorus of bright gold stars. The fine, grass-like foliage persists until early summer and must be allowed to die down naturally. This is one of the least expensive, early-flowering crocuses so you don't have to be rich to create a bold patch, close to a path or at a strategic point where you can see it from a window. It settles down readily in any open, well-drained situation and increases rapidly when given the benefit of maximum sunshine. A liquid feed after flowering helps to ensure a bright display the following year.

 2 ○ ◆

Crocus sieberi and Crocus tomasinianus

C.sieberi
'Violet Queen'

C.sieberi
'Hubert Edelsten'

C.tomasinianus
'Albus'

C.tomasinianus
Whitewell Purple'

Two more early-flowering **Crocus** species which are very suitable for making patches of colour on a lawn or at the edge of a border. *C.sieberi* cultivars include the deservedly popular 'Violet Queen', the huge purple and white 'Hubert Edelsten', and the pale blue and gold 'Atticus'. The most freely available *C.tomasinianus* cultivar is the large flowered reddish-mauve 'Whitewell Purple', but the white 'Albus' and lavender and purple 'Pictus' are worth snapping up if you see them offered. Both species are perfectly happy in any sunny, well-drained soil, but if you plant them in the lawn then you must mow round them until the foliage dies down in June.

 2–3 ○ ◆

WINTER

Cyclamen coum

C.coum

This charming Turkish alpine **Cyclamen** begins to flower in December and gradually, over several weeks, produces a profusion of tiny blooms which can be anything from a delicate pink to deep crimson depending on which form you have obtained. The tubers should be planted about 5cm (2in) deep and 10cm (4in) apart in full sun or light shade. The plants look well close to the edge of a path or at the base of a small tree, and never grow more than 5cm (2in) tall. The flowers are followed by a carpet of flat, dark green leaves, sometimes beautifully veined or marbled with silver. *C.orbiculatum,* *C.hiemale, C.ibericum, C.vernum* and *C.atkinsii* are now generally considered to be forms of *C.coum* rather than distinct species.

 12–2

Daphne mezereum

D.mezereum

This sweetly scented little shrub is deservedly popular. **Daphne** thrives in sun or semi-shade and is particularly happy on chalky soil. Apart from the usual purple flowered form there are white and pink cultivars 'Alba' and 'Rosea' but these are not so widely offered. This species rarely grows more than 150cm (5ft) tall and is usually as wide as it is high. The flowers are succeeded by brightly coloured berries which are poisonous and should be picked off if they are within reach of small children. The shrub is not long lived but new plants can easily be grown from seed gathered and sown in mid-summer.

 2–3

WINTER

Elaeagnus pungens 'Maculata'

'Maculata'

This vigorous, compact evergreen makes an excellent wind-resistant screen and thrives in an open position in any fertile garden soil. Most forms of *E.pungens* are variegated but the large central gold splash on the leaves of 'Maculata' is particularly striking and, coupled with its moderate, steady growth, makes it the most popular. It rarely exceeds 3m (10ft) tall by 2m (6½ft) across but care should be taken to prune out any shoots which have only plain green leaves before such shoots become dominant and the dazzling green and gold winter effect is lost. The small white, fragrant flowers produced in autumn are another good reason for planting this handsome shrub.

Eranthis hyemalis

E.hyemalis

The **Winter Aconite** is valued for its carpet of brilliant, golden flowers beneath deciduous trees or in moist, shaded corners. The knobbly tubers should be planted in September or October about 5cm (2in) deep and preferably in groups of five or ten. Alternatively, if you are able to buy plants 'in the green' in March or April, plant them immediately in moist soil to die down naturally as the summer progresses. On no account disturb the tubers except just after flowering and then only very occasionally. A good mulch of well-rotted leafmould or compost in late summer ensures a consistently brilliant display.

2–3

WINTER

Erica × darleyensis

'Arthur
Johnson'

'Silberschmelze'

'Darley Dale'

These handsome **Heathers**, hybrids between *E.carnea* and *E.mediterranea*, are lime-tolerant like their parents but even so they may not succeed on very shallow, chalky soils. Most cultivars form a hemispherical mound about 50cm (20in) across and flower profusely right through the winter in an open sunny spot. Their foliage provides dense, weedproof ground cover for the rest of the year. 'Arthur Johnson' is a very popular and reliable cultivar and probably the longest flowering of all, with sprays of magenta flowers from early December until April. The best white cultivar is 'Silberschmelze' which has sweetly scented flowers. The most popular pink is 'Darley Dale'.

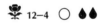 12–4 ○ ◖◗

Fatsia japonica

F.japonica

If left alone, the **False Castor Oil Plant** will, after ten or twelve years, make a large, spreading shrub up to 4m (13ft) tall and 5m (16ft) across. Its huge, hand-shaped, glossy green leaves are often as much as 35cm (14in) across. It is an unbeatable plant for foliage effect in a shaded or semi-shaded spot and the October display of globular flowerheads gives it an even more exotic appearance as winter approaches. It will succeed in any good garden soil and is excellent for seaside gardens. Pruning of dead or unwanted shoots should be done only in spring. The intriguing hybrid between this plant and the common ivy, × *fatshedera*, is lower growing and less hardy.

 10–11 ● ◖◗◗

WINTER

Galanthus nivalis

'Sam Arnott'

Atkinsii'

'Plena'

Snowdrops come in all shapes and sizes and thrive in moist, lightly shaded soils. The most common species is *G.nivalis* which flowers in February and March, and many named cultivars, including double flowered ones, are offered. They vary in height from 10cm to 20cm (4–8in) and some flower earlier than others. The cultivar 'Sam Arnott' has a pleasing scent if picked and brought indoors and 'Atkinsii' which flowers slightly earlier is also very handsome. Both are about 20cm (8in) tall. The double flowered 'Plena' is about 10cm (4in) tall. Established clumps can be divided and replanted immediately after flowering every three years if desired.

 2–3

Garrya elliptica

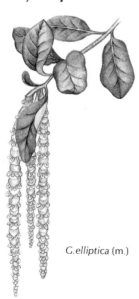

G.elliptica (m.)

In very cold districts this handsome evergreen is best grown against a wall, but in other areas will do equally well on a north- or east-facing wall, or as a free-standing shrub. It is tolerant of coastal winds and atmospheric pollution, and succeeds readily in any fertile well-drained soil. In January and February the shrub is hung with beautiful grey-green catkins. The male plant is considered to have the better catkins and the clone 'James Roof' has especially long ones, but those on the female are almost equally attractive. After twenty years a good specimen should be at its full height of 5m (16ft) with a spread of 3m (10ft).

 2 ● ♦♦

WINTER

Hamamelis mollis

'Pallida'

The **Chinese Witch Hazel** makes a very attractive shrub or small tree and will grow readily in most rich, moist soils except where there is a high proportion of lime or chalk. If planted close to a path or in a lawn, the spidery yellow flowers, which appear from late December to early March, can be properly seen and, what is more to the point, smelled. They have a sweet, delicate, teasing perfume. Witch hazels are slow growing, usually reaching only 2.5m (8ft) tall after twenty years but eventually attaining a height of between 5m and 8m (16—26ft). The form 'Pallida' has particularly large, dense flowers and golden autumn foliage.

🌹 12—3   ◐   ●●

Hedera helix

'Gold Heart'

'Cristata'

'Buttercup'

The **Common Ivy** is probably the most versatile evergreen climber available to gardeners and the choice of cultivars is enormous. You can get curly-edged leaves like 'Cristata', variegated ones like 'Gold Heart', golden-leafed ones like 'Buttercup' and any number of plain, green-leafed ones. They are utterly unfussy as to situation and completely undemanding as to soil type. If allowed to clothe a brick wall they will, provided that the brickwork and pointing is sound in the first place, form a protective, insulating layer and cause no damage whatsoever. They also make first-class weed-smothering ground cover on awkward banks and inaccessible corners.

●   ●●

27

WINTER

Hedera colchica

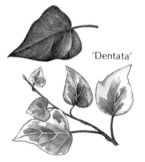

'Dentata'

'Dentata Variegata'

'Paddy's Pride'

The **Persian Ivy** has much larger, bolder foliage than its cousin *H.helix* and is useful in situations where there is a large surface area to cover. The largest leaves of all belong to the cultivar 'Dentata' and her variegated sister 'Dentata Variegata', the latter being spectacularly patterned with grey, creamy-yellow and near-white. 'Paddy's Pride' with its central splash of yellow, merging into pale green and then deep green at the margin, is also very popular. All cultivars are as easy to grow as *H.helix* but good light is needed for the variegation to develop to its best effect. Trained over chain-link fencing or wooden palings, *H.colchica* makes an interesting and unusual hedge.

◐ ♦♦♦

Helleborus corsicus and Helleborus niger

H.corsicus

H.niger

The **Corsican Hellebore** makes a 60cm (24in) tall clump of grey-green foliage, surmounted in late winter by large heads of apple-green flowers. It enjoys a shaded, well-drained spot in rich soil and appreciates an occasional top dressing of well-rotted manure. If you must divide the clumps then do so only in March because they hate being disturbed at any other time. The shorter *H.niger*, the **Christmas Rose**, will seldom attain a height of more than 40cm (16in) and should be given the same treatment as *H.corsicus*. In December its white, saucer-shaped flowers and deep green foliage make a delightful picture at the front of a shrubbery or against a north-facing wall.

🌺 2 ● ♦♦♦

Ilex × *altaclarensis* and *Ilex aquifolium*

'J.C. van Tol'

'Golden King'

'Silver Queen'

The **Holly** tolerates almost any soil, provided there is a fair amount of moisture available, and doesn't seem to mind whether it grows in sun or shade. It makes an effective hedge, and as a specimen in a lawn or at the end of a terrace the variegated cultivars are especially handsome. Careful training in the early years will eventually give you a medium-sized tree anything up to 20m (66ft) tall with about 2m (6½ft) of clear trunk; but being extremely slow growing it will take some twenty years before you have a specimen even 5m (16ft) tall. Most of the named cultivars commercially offered are either *I.* × *altaclarensis* hybrids or else *I.aquifolium* hybrids but there is confusion as to which of these two groups some belong. The magnificent dark green 'J.C. van Tol', probably the most reliable berry-bearing cultivar, is found under × *altaclarensis* in some catalogues and under *aquifolium* in others, but since the two groups are substantially the same for garden purposes the distinction is usually ignored. The gender of some cultivars is also confusing: the beautifully variegated 'Golden King' is female; the strikingly marbled and white-edged 'Silver Queen' is male. To ensure a crop of berries on female plants you must have a male in reasonably close proximity. The best time for planting hollies is March or April and it is essential that the plant is kept well-watered right through its first summer.

Iris danfordiae

I.danfordiae

Dwarf Irises make a brief but beautiful display at the edge of a path or on a rockery. *Iris danfordiae* is very popular for its deep, golden-yellow flowers, standing about 12cm (5½ in) tall, which emerge before the foliage. They like a chalky, well-drained soil and if your soil is acid then a dressing of lime should be given when planting and periodically thereafter. If planted about 15cm (6in) deep in a moist semi-shaded spot they will normally flower each January but not increase very rapidly. If planted about only 5cm (2in) deep they will flower the first year after planting and then the bulb will divide into several small bulblets which, with the correct feeding and careful attention, can be grown on to flowering size.

 1–2 ◑ ◆◆◆

Iris reticulata

'Cantab'

The other favourite **Dwarf Iris** is *Iris reticulata*. It prefers a fairly moist position in sun or light shade. Again it is partial to lime and some should be added if it is being planted in acid soil. Apart from the original species with its deep mauve flowers delicately marked with rich golden splashes, a number of named cultivars is available. The most frequently offered is 'Cantab'. Others range in colour from the sky-blue and gold 'Harmony' to the sweet-smelling, reddish-purple 'J.S.Dijt'. All grow to about 15cm (6in) tall and should be planted between 10cm and 15cm (4—6in) deep in groups of ten or more.

 2–3 ◑ ◆◆

WINTER

Jasminum nudiflorum

J.nudiflorum

Winter Jasmine is an attractive, easy-going, winter-flowering shrub. It is usually grown against a wall but is equally effective for covering a sloping bank or as a graceful, free-standing shrub. It is at home on any kind of soil and facing any point of the compass, although an east wall is unsuitable where morning sunshine on frosted flowers will spoil the blossom. Strong shoots should be pruned back by about one-third as soon as they have finished flowering. Weaker flowering shoots should be pruned back to the old wood. The plant can reach as high as 3m (10ft) tall against a wall and a spread of up to 2m (6½ft) but annual pruning can keep it smaller if desired.

 1–3 ○ ♦♦

Juniperus horizontalis

'Glauca'

'Emerald Spreader'

The prostrate **Creeping Juniper** is a most effective evergreen ground-cover plant for open or lightly shaded areas. The foliage colours of various cultivars range from the steel-blue of 'Glauca' and its slightly more silvery kinsman 'Wiltonii' (sometimes offered as 'Blue Rug'), to the brilliant, emerald green of 'Emerald Spreader'. Depending on the cultivar you will find that after about ten years the shrub will have a spread of anywhere between 1m and 2m (3¼–6½ft) and none stands more than 20cm (8in) high. Some cultivars such as 'Prince of Wales' turn a rich, purplish-brown in winter. All are lime-tolerant and perfectly hardy.

○ ♦♦

WINTER

Laurus nobilis

L.nobilis

The **Bay Tree** is a very handsome evergreen which makes a dense hedge or specimen shrub. It will, if left unpruned, reach a height of about 6m (20ft) within twenty years, forming an elegant pyramid some 3m (10ft) at the base. It is often clipped into all sorts of shapes. Any fertile, well-drained soil will suit it and it thrives in coastal areas. Frost-damaged shoots should be pruned out in March and, if desired, a second pruning can be given in August. Sprays of foilage cut for culinary use should be hung up in a cool, airy place to dry for at least four weeks before being stored in an airtight jar or tin.

◑ ◆◆

Lonicera × purpusii

L. × purpusii

Of the winter-flowering shrubby **Honeysuckles**, this vigorous, attractive hybrid between *L.fragrantissima* and *L.standishii* is probably the best garden plant. Like its parents it is semi-evergreen and easily grown in sun or light shade in any garden soil. The small, creamy-white blossoms in January and February have a delicious perfume. It makes a columnar shrub of about 150cm (5ft) tall by about 150cm across. Unless you particularly want the display of glossy red berries that follow in May, you should prune the flowering shoots back to within 5cm (2in) of the old wood as soon as the flowers have faded. A few vigorous shoots may be left to bear their berries and pruned out the following year.

🌺 1–2 ◑ ◆◆

WINTER

Mahonia × media 'Charity'

'Charity'

The **Mahonias** are a first-class evergreen subject for shaded or semi-shaded positions on any well-drained soil, chalk included. 'Charity' is a striking, compact clone of the × media group of hybrids between *M.japonica* and *M.lomariifolia*, which will ultimately make a dome-shaped specimen about 2m (6½ft) high and a little over 150cm (5ft) across but larger in some instances. The star-shaped sprays of tiny, fragrant, pale-yellow flowers are borne at the ends of the branches and present an attractive sight in December and January. The blue-black berries which follow in early summer are edible. Indeed, those of some species are used for jam-making.

 12–1

Myrica cerifera

M.cerifera

This attractive, North American evergreen shrub is nicknamed the **Wax Myrtle** or **Candleberry** because the glaucous wax which coats the berries can be made into fragrant candles (but you do need plenty of berries for even one decent-sized candle). The narrow foliage is also sweetly fragrant so the fact that the small catkins which appear in February or March are of no special beauty does not seem too important. It thrives best in semi-shade on very moist, acid soil and in the right boggy conditions will attain a height of up to 6m (20ft) and a spread of about 2m (6½ft). Although not frequently offered, it is well worth tracking down if you have the right spot for it.

 2

WINTER

Pachysandra terminalis

'Variegata'

The **Japanese Spurge** is an extremely useful ground-hugging evergreen shrub which will happily carpet bare patches under trees and in shaded corners. It tolerates any soil type but is less vigorous on shallow, chalky ones, and it is surprisingly resistant to summer drought. The greenish-white flowers appear in February and March above the attractive diamond-shaped foliage. Many nurseries and garden centres offer a variegated form with attractive white mottling and this form is just as tolerant of dry shade as its plain green sister. Once planted it can be left to spread itself or helped along by dividing the plants after flowering in spring.

 2–3

Picea abies 'Nidiformis'

'Nidiformis'

The best known **Norway Spruce** is, of course, the one sold as Christmas trees, but a great number of dwarf and slow-growing forms have arisen which are unfussy as to soil type and well suited to an open position on the rock garden or in an island bed in a lawn or patio. Many produce attractive lime-green shoots in spring when the new season's growth commences. *P.abies* 'Nidiformis' is particularly popular for this reason. It will attain less than 50cm (20in) in height even after thirty years with a spread of around 2m (6½ft). Erect, dome-shaped and prostrate cultivars also exist which share the attractive foliage and slow-growing habit of 'Nidiformis'.

WINTER

Pinus radiata

For a medium or large garden in need of a good-sized, fast-growing specimen evergreen, the **Monterey Pine** must be the answer. Tolerant of any soil and highly wind-resistant it will quickly assume a mature appearance, attaining anything up to 20m (66ft) in height within twenty years with a head some 6m (20ft) across. The main trunk at this age would be clear of branches for at least the first 4m (13ft). When buying, always choose a small specimen, certainly no more than 45cm (18in) tall. They hate being transplanted except when very young. It is also most unwise to move the tree once it is established, for the chances are it would simply die.

P.radiata

 ○ ◆◆◆ ●

Prunus subhirtella 'Autumnalis'

Although most cultivars of *Prunus subhirtella* bloom in early spring, 'Autumnalis' (**Autumn Cherry**) will produce its pretty white flowers intermittently from November right through to March. It makes an attractive small tree, rarely more than 7m (22½ft) tall, with a dense twiggy crown 3m or 4m (10—13ft) across. It is at home on any soil but, like other cherries, does particularly well on chalky soils. A pink flowered form 'Autumnalis Rosea' is also frequently available. Both often display very handsome red and bronze foliage in autumn. Cutting sprays of blossom for indoor decoration does not harm the tree once it is established.

'Autumnalis'

 ❀ 11–2 ○ ◆◆

WINTER

Rhododendron 'Praecox'

'Praecox'

True to its name, this attractive, compact, low-growing hybrid usually begins to flower in February and sometimes even earlier in the mild south-west of England. The purple-crimson buds open to an attractive rosy-crimson funnel shape and are borne in twos or threes at the tips of the shoots. The small, dark green leaves are fragrant when crushed between finger and thumb, and in very cold districts the plant sometimes adopts a semi-deciduous habit instead of remaining evergreen all through the winter. The plant will thrive in any lime-free soil in sun or light shade and will rarely grow taller than 80cm (2¾ft) or spread wider than 75cm (30in).

 3

Rosmarinus officinalis

R. officinalis

Although valued for its use in the kitchen, the **Common Rosemary** is often overlooked as a potential garden shrub in its own right. This attractive, grey-green low-growing evergreen is, for instance, useful as a small hedge, and in winter would make an excellent background to early-flowering bulbs or hellebores. Even under ideal conditions it never reaches more than 2m (6½ft) tall and with light pruning in early summer can be maintained at a much smaller level, say 80cm (2¾ft) high and 40cm (16in) across. It prefers open, well-drained soils in full sun and is lime-tolerant. As an alternative to dwarf conifers it is certainly an evergreen well worth considering.

 4–11

WINTER

Sarcococca humilis

S. humilis

This dwarf species of **Christmas Box** will form itself into a dense, twiggy evergreen, reaching about 60cm (24in) high. As an individual plant it would probably attain a spread of about 80cm (2¾ ft) but its habit of sending up suckers from its roots enables it to spread much further if allowed to do so. Being fairly slow growing, it is some years before its spread causes any problem. The tiny, white, sweetly scented flowers usually open in February and look charming if sprays are cut and arranged with jasmine or forsythia. The plant will be happy in shade or semi-shade on any fertile garden soil but is especially suited to chalk or lime.

 2

Scilla tubergeniana

S. tubergeniana

This delightful, early-flowering bulb makes a pretty patch of bluish-white flowers in February. The flower spikes are usually quite short at first but gradually extend to between 10cm and 15cm (4–6in) as the flowers open up. The bulbs should be planted as soon as they are obtained, about 7cm (2¾ in) deep and 7cm apart in groups of four or five. In full sun or semi-shade the plants will increase themselves readily and if clumps become congested they can be lifted and divided in late summer once the foliage has died down. They are quite undemanding as to soil type but appreciate a liquid feed after flowering.

 2

WINTER

Senecio cineraria

S.cineraria

Although frequently treated as a half-hardy annual in summer bedding schemes, the **Sea Ragwort,** often sold as *Cineraria maritima,* is actually reasonably hardy. In a sheltered, semi-shaded corner of a city or seaside garden its striking rosettes of silver foliage create a most unusual effect in winter and early spring. The yellow flowers which appear in summer are not really very attractive and can be removed to encourage the production of more foliage. When the plants become too straggly, cuttings can be taken in spring but should spend the first winter under glass before being planted out the following year in place of their exhausted predecessors.

Sternbergia candida

S.candida

This unusual species is still fairly new to commerce and may prove difficult and expensive to obtain for some years yet, but it will surely prove to be a popular and permanent addition to the winter garden. Like other *Sternbergia* species it requires well-drained soil in full sun, and in acid soils a dressing of lime is appreciated. The large, white, sweetly scented crocus-shaped flowers emerge in January or early February and, when fully developed, stand some 15cm (6in) tall. The bulbs should be planted about 5cm (2in) deep and 10cm (4in) apart.

 1–2 ○ ◆

WINTER

Thuja orientalis 'Aurea Nana'

Cultivars of *T.orientalis* come in all shapes and sizes but they include a wide choice of dwarf and slow-growing kinds suitable for the rock garden or heather garden. 'Aurea Nana' is a most attractive golden-green and forms a compact, oval bush some 75cm (30in) tall after ten years. It continues to grow very slowly for many years after that. The foliage is delightfully aromatic. It thrives in an open position on any well-drained soil. *T.orientalis* 'Conspicua' has a similar colour but grows taller, reaching about 2m (6½ft) in ten years, while 'Elegantissima' is similar in habit and colour to 'Conspicua' but turns an attractive greeny-bronze in winter.

'Aurea Nana'

○ ◗◗

Viburnum × bodnantense

'Dawn'

This beautiful medium-sized shrub produces clusters of tiny, sweet-smelling flowers over a long period, often beginning in November and continuing to open two or three heads at each mild spell until March. It will eventually attain a height of about 3m (10ft) and a spread of 150cm (5ft), and prefers a position in full sun. The two clones most frequently offered are 'Dawn' and 'Debon' and, frankly, there is little to choose between them. Each is very floriferous, superbly fragrant and an excellent garden plant, at home on any fertile garden soil. The two parents of this handsome hybrid, *V.farreri* and *V.grandiflorum*, are also excellent winter-flowering shrubs in their own right.

❀ 11–3 ○ ◗◗

SPRING

The main feature of the spring display in most gardens is the flowering bulbs, especially crocus, daffodils and tulips, and the early-flowering shrubs and trees — camellias and rhododendrons if your garden has acid soil, ornamental quinces, daphnes and flowering cherries if you are on neutral or alkaline soil. The garden seems suddenly to come awake again and numerous tasks present themselves; the pruning of roses, buddleias and other shrubs that flower on new wood, the clearing away of dead flower stems and seedheads of astilbes, sedums and achillea and the general tidying up of last year's spent growth in the herbaceous border. Those plants that benefit from the application of a general purpose fertilizer, such as paeonies, lilies and delphiniums, should be thoroughly dosed and a light mulch of compost should then be spread over the emerging shoots. In many cases this is the best time to plant or replant those sites that you intend to change and garden centres and stores are bursting with new trees, shrubs and herbaceous plants as well as a huge selection of tools and equipment. This really is the best time to buy, but don't overdo it; buy only what you can cope with in a couple of weeks, because plants purchased and then left standing around in their pots or packaging will deteriorate rapidly at this time of the year.

SPRING

Achillea 'Moonshine'

'Moonshine'

This bright yellow hybrid is the earliest of its group to bloom, opening its flat, plate-like heads of yellow flowers in mid-May. These remain, without fading, for several weeks and if they are cut back in July and the foliage trimmed, a second flowering can often be induced in early autumn. The feathery, silvery-green foliage is present all year round and is an attractive feature in its own right. Like other achilleas it thrives best in a sunny, well-drained spot but tolerates any fertile garden soil. Its other attraction is that, being somewhat shorter than its later-flowering siblings, only 60cm (24in) tall at the most, it does not require staking.

 4–6 ○ ◗

Adonis vernalis

A. vernalis

This species of **Adonis** is taller and later flowering than *A.amurensis* described on page 19. It too enjoys an open or semi-shaded position and is tolerant of any soil type. The glistening, golden-yellow flowerheads stand some 40cm (16in) tall and appear during April and May above the mound of soft green, feathery foliage that is common to most species of this genus. The whole of the plant visible above ground vanishes completely in early autumn and re-emerges as a group of fat buds only a month or so before it is ready to flower again. At the front of a border it gives a touch of brightness before the summer-flowering perennials begin to bloom.

 4–5 ○ ◗◗

SPRING

Ajuga reptans

'Atropurpurea'

The **Common Bugle** is a very useful ground-carpeting plant which sends up compact spikes of dark blue flowers from April to early June. The species commonly found in most British woodlands has plain, dark green leaves which form a spreading clump about 10cm (4in) high in any shady, moist corner. Some interesting coloured-leafed forms have arisen such as the purple-leafed 'Atropurpurea' and the astonishing pink, bronze and purple-leafed 'Tricolour'. These are very popular but need more light, otherwise the colouring reverts to dull green. As a rule of thumb, the paler and more complex the colouring of the leaves, the more light they require.

 4–6

Alyssum saxatile

'Citrinum'

For most of the year this plant is a spreading, 20cm (8in) tall mound of soft, oval, grey foliage, but in April it suddenly vanishes beneath a dense mass of tiny yellow flowers borne in round clusters on short, grey stalks. It requires a well-drained spot in full sun but is utterly unfussy as to soil type. The primrose-yellow flowers of the cultivar 'Citrinum' (sometimes sold as 'Silver Queen') make it a firm favourite but the charming buff-yellow 'Dudley Neville' and the deep golden, double flowered 'Flore Pleno' are also very popular. To prevent them from becoming straggly and untidy, weak or unwanted shoots should be snipped out immediately after flowering.

 4

43

SPRING

Arabis albida

A.albida

Once you see a broad, mature mat of this plant in full bloom, you really appreciate its nickname **Snow-in-Summer**. It forms a spreading mound of silvery-grey foliage about 12cm (5½ in) high, but in late April this is submerged beneath a froth of dazzling white flowers. The plant is very partial to lime and, in an open sunny spot at the edge of a path or spilling over a low retaining wall, will form a thick mat anything up to 100cm (3¼ ft) across although its tendency to become somewhat straggly usually encourages a good tidying-up with the kitchen scissors as soon as it has finished flowering. Pink and double flowered cultivars are sometimes offered.

 5 ◯ ◗

Armeria maritima

'Düsseldorf Pride'

The **Sea Pink** is frequently found in a sunny, well-drained spot on a rockery or in a trough garden as a treasured memento of a seaside holiday. It is of course also widely known as **Thrift** and adorned the back of a threepenny piece in pre-decimal days. The grass-like, evergreen foliage forms a slow-growing hummock, seldom more than 10cm (4in) high. The flowerheads are held drumstick fashion above the leaves, between 15cm and 25cm (6—8in) tall. Colours vary from the warm, crimson-pink of 'Vindictive' and 'Düsseldorf Pride' to the pure white 'Alba', with every shade of pink in between.

 5 ◯ ◗

SPRING

Arnebia echioides

The **Prophet Flower** is an intriguing perennial which succeeds easily in any sunny, well-drained spot but is grateful for the addition of a handful of grit or sharp sand mixed into the soil before planting. The narrow leaves form neat mounds about 20cm (8in) high and in April the flower stems emerge from the centre of the mound, each bearing several buds. These open into clear yellow trumpets with a chocolate-coloured dot at the base of each petal which gradually disappears as the flower matures. New plants can easily be grown from seed collected in late summer and sown in a quick-draining seed compost the following spring.

A.echioides

 4–5 ○ ◗

Arum italicum 'Marmoratum' ('Pictum')

'Marmoratum'

It is difficult to know in which season *A.italicum* is at its most interesting. In late autumn the dark green, arrow-shaped leaves with beautiful white marbling emerge forming an attractive focus in a moist, shady or semi-shaded corner. The 20cm (8in) high greenish-white flowers in late spring are often discounted as an attraction but their cool colour in a period alive with brilliant yellows and gaudy reds has much to be said for it. The spikes of dazzling scarlet berries appearing in September are also extremely handsome. The tubers should be planted 8cm (3in) deep and 20cm (8in) apart in groups of five or ten. It needs a year or two to establish itself.

 4

SPRING

Aubrieta deltoidea

'Dr Mules'

Aubrieta is available in numerous shades of wine-red, purple, blue and pink and forms mats of glowing colour from late March to the end of May. Being too invasive for the average rock garden it is best planted at the edge of a path or overhanging a low retaining wall in full sun. In mid-June it should be dead-headed with a pair of shears or a strimmer and straggly growths trimmed off to maintain a neat cushion shape. A good plant will eventually attain a spread of up to 100cm (3¼ft). Named clones such as the deep violet 'Dr Mules', the light pink 'Maurice Pritchard' or the wine-coloured 'Red Carpet' are deservedly popular choices from a very wide range.

 3–5

Berberis darwinii

B.darwinii

This attractive but prickly-leafed, spring-flowering evergreen is one of the most easily grown garden shrubs to be found. In April and May the long sprays of crimson-tipped yellow flowers contrast superbly with the glossy, dark green foliage. It will thrive in all types of garden soil except those which become heavily waterlogged, and is equally at home in sun or shade. Within twenty years it will attain its full height of about 2.5m (8ft) and a spread of 1.5m (5ft). The heavy clusters of blue-black berries that follow the flowers are an additional attraction. This species is named after Charles Darwin and was discovered in Chile during the voyage of the *Beagle* in 1835.

 4–5

SPRING

Berberis × stenophylla

'Semperflorens'

This attractive evergreen hybrid between *B.darwinii* and *B.empetrifolia* has given rise to a number of interestingly ornamental cultivars. All flower profusely in April or May but 'Autumnalis' will produce a second flush of bloom in September and, being fairly small — about 150cm (5ft) tall by 100cm (3¼ft) — is often preferred for a small garden. 'Corallina Compacta' is a dwarf, rarely exceeding 30cm (12in) tall by 45cm (18in) across even after many years. 'Semperflorens' is of a similar size and habit to 'Autumnalis' but continues to flower well into June or July. In each case the flower buds are a rich orange-crimson opening to a warm deep yellow.

 4–5 ◑ ♦♦

Berberis thunbergii

'Helmond'

'Aurea'

Of the deciduous **Barberries**, the cultivars of *B.thunbergii* are among the most frequently offered. The pale, straw-yellow flowers which cover the shrub in April and May are displayed against a wide variety of foliage colours. 'Atropurpurea' when mature is nearly 2m (6½ft) tall and about 120cm (4ft) across with rich bronzy-purple foliage that turns a brilliant red in autumn. 'Helmond' has similar colouring but a much narrower silhouette, usually attaining a height of about 180cm (6ft) but rarely more than 60cm (24in) across. 'Aurea' has beautiful lime-green foliage on reddish-brown stems. All are happy in sun or shade and tolerant of any soil.

 4–5 ◑ ♦♦

SPRING

Bergenia cordifolia

B.cordifolia

You have only to look at the leaves of this striking perennial to understand why it is called **Elephants' Ears**. In sun or shade the fleshy, dark green foliage forms a rich pattern, each plant being 40cm or 50cm (16—20in) across and about 25cm (10in) high. The large sprays of rosy-pink flowers which emerge in April and May often seem too heavy for their rather lax stems and droop above the foliage. The leaves of the cultivar 'Purpurea' turn a rich bronze-purple in winter. The hybrid 'Silberlicht' (usually offered as 'Silver Light') is a popular white flowered cultivar and blooms slightly earlier.

Brunnera macrophylla

'Langtrees'

The dense heart-shaped foliage of this delightful East European perennial makes excellent ground cover in moist, semi-shaded areas. From April to June, dainty sprays of tiny blue flowers cluster on 40cm (16in) tall stems (often mistaken for Forget-me-nots) to form a delicate pattern. They are also delightful to cut and arrange. A variegated cultivar 'Variegata' with strikingly patterned leaves of primrose-yellow and green is fairly widely available; 'Langtrees', a speckled-leafed cultivar with a rim of pale green splashes round the border of the leaf, can also occasionally be obtained. All are fairly vigorous but rapid spread can be promoted by dividing the plants in September.

SPRING

Caltha palustris

C.palustris

C.palustris 'Plena'

The common name of this plant is **Marsh Marigold** which obviously indicates that it must have moist or boggy soil in an open, sunny position. The clumps of glossy green foliage are usually about 15cm (6in) high and 30cm (12in) across when fully developed. After the heart-shaped leaves have appeared in early spring they are almost obscured in April and May by the brilliant, golden-yellow flowerheads. As well as the single flowered form there is also a double C.palustris 'Plena' and it is also often possible to obtain a white (C.palustris 'Alba'). To increase your stock simply divide the clumps and replant immediately after flowering.

🌺 4–5 ◑ 💧💧💧

Camellia × williamsii

'Donation'

'J.C. Williams'

This group of hybrids between C.japonica and C.saluenensis was initiated by J.C. Williams at Caerhays Castle in Cornwall in the 1920s. They have handsome evergreen foliage and flower over a very long period, often commencing in November and continuing right through to May. In moist, lime-free soil they will attain a height and spread of up to 2m (6½ft) square within ten years. Among the most popular cultivars are the semi-double, orchid-pink 'Donation' and the rich pink single 'J.C. Williams'. Be sure to plant where they will not catch the morning sun or the blossoms will be scorched and blemished in frosty weather.

🌺 12–4 ◑ 💧💧💧

SPRING

Camellia japonica

'Lady Vansittart'

'Drama Girl'

'Alba Simplex'

The **Camellias** most frequently found in gardens are cultivars of *C. japonica*. The original wild species was introduced to the UK in 1739 but it had been known and cultivated for over 2,000 years in China and Japan. It ranges from pure white to a red so dark it seems almost black and from graceful single blooms to the intricate formal doubles. You may find your own plants producing odd blooms of a distinctly different colour from the ones on the rest of the bush: these are known as sports. If the shoot is taken from the bush and rooted after flowering it will normally grow into a new plant bearing all of its flowers identical to the sport, although some plants propagated in this fashion do revert to type.

There are many cultivars to choose from. Most will make a shrub some 2m (6½ft) tall and 150cm (5ft) across after ten years but will grow slowly thereafter. The flowers usually bloom from February to April. Most nurseries and garden centres will at least offer the following plants and usually more besides: 'Mathotiana Alba', a handsome white formal double and its equally lovely pink sister 'Mathotiana Rosea'; the blood-red semi-double 'Adolphe Audusson'; the pink and white striped 'Lady Vansittart'; the elegant white, single flowered 'Devonia'; and the deep rose-pink 'Drama Girl'. As with *C. × williamsii*, these shrubs thrive on lime-free soil in a semi-shaded position out of the way of the early morning sun.

🏵 2–4 ◑ ♦♦♦

Chaenomeles japonica

C. *japonica*

Most of the **Japanese Quinces** bear flowers from March to May, but if grown against a sheltering west-facing wall they will often bloom earlier. *C. japonica* is a small, thorny, deciduous shrub about 100cm (3¼ft) tall with a spread of about 150cm (5ft). The flame-orange, saucer-shaped flowers often begin to open before the leaves are fully developed, and in autumn you will find a crop of golden-yellow fruits which can be made into a jelly every bit as good as that obtained from the true quince, *Cydonia oblonga*. The shrub is easily cultivated on any good garden soil and will grow equally well in sun or semi-shade.

 3–5

Chaenomeles speciosa

'Moerloesii'

'Simonii'

Most cultivars of this handsome species of **Japanese Quince** tend to be relatively tall. The pure-white flowered 'Nivalis' will make a specimen of up to 3m (10ft) tall by 2m (6½ft) across when trained on a north- or east-facing wall, while the pink and white 'Moerloesii' will reach 150cm (5ft) tall by 2m (6½ft) across in the same situation (this cultivar is sometimes offered as 'Apple Blossom'). The blood-red 'Simonii' is dwarf with semi-double flowers. All are completely at home on any good garden soil. Once established they should be carefully pruned back to the old wood in late winter of each year, except for the leading shoots which should be shortened back to a bud at about one-third the length.

 3–5

Chaenomeles × superba

'Pink Lady'

These attractive **Flowering Quinces** are hybrids between C.japonica and C.speciosa. Their colours range from the brilliant sealing-wax red of 'Rowallane' to the modest rose-pink of 'Pink Lady'. None of the cultivars usually offered for sale will grow much more than 150cm (5ft) tall by 150cm in diameter but some, such as 'Pink Lady' and her bright red sister 'Fire Dance', spread themselves by means of suckers and, if left uncontrolled, might swamp less vigorous neighbours. Like the parent plants, these hybrids flower on old wood so the new growth should be pruned back in late winter to form flowering spurs. They grow well in sun or semi-shade on any fertile garden soil.

 4–5 ◑ ♦♦

Cheiranthus cheiri

'Harpur Crewe'

'Wenlock Beauty'

'Moonlight'

Not all **Wallflowers** are biennial plants. This group is perennial and well worth considering for an open, sunny, well-drained spot. Wallflowers are partial to a small amount of lime in the soil, so if yours is acid add a handful when planting. The double, golden-yellow 'Harpur Crewe' is beautifully scented and a firm favourite with many gardeners. It grows about 40cm (16in) tall as does the mauve and gold 'Constant Cheer'. 'Wenlock Beauty', a striking coppery-red, and the warm orange 'Rufus' grow only about 20cm (8in) tall. The even lower growing 'Moonlight', rarely more than 10cm (4in) tall, is sometimes offered as Erysimum alpinus.

 4 ○ ♦

SPRING

Chionodoxa

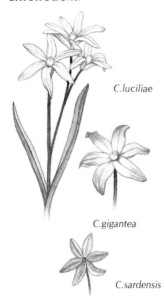

C.luciliae

C.gigantea

C.sardensis

The **Glory of the Snow** is a lovely sight in its Turkish mountain homeland as it raises its brilliant blue flowers above the melting snow at the end of winter. It is also one of the easiest of garden bulbs and naturalizes readily in any sunny, well-drained spot. The species commercially offered are completely unfussy as to soil type, bloom in March or early April, grow about 15cm (6in) tall and multiply rapidly if given a liquid feed after flowering. *C.luciliae* has sky-blue flowers with a white centre and there is also a pink form. *C.gigantea* has large, lilac-blue flowers and *C.sardensis* is a true royal blue. Plant them in bold clumps about 8cm (3in) deep with the bulbs 4cm (1 ¾ in) apart.

 3 ○

Convallaria majalis

The graceful, exquisitely scented sprays of **Lily of the Valley** are a delight to discover in a moist shady corner of your garden. Out of doors they bloom in late April and May but a few roots lifted and potted up in autumn can be forced into flower in a warm greenhouse or on a warm north-facing window sill to make a sweet-smelling Mother's Day gift. The plants are usually about 15cm (6in) tall and the spear-shaped leaves make excellent ground cover through the summer. They respond well to an autumn dressing of lime but otherwise prefer to be left alone.

 4–5 ●

C.majalis

SPRING

Coronilla glauca

C.glauca

The primrose-yellow flowers and soft grey foliage of this delightful shrub look especially attractive in April and early May, but it will continue to produce the odd spray of blossom throughout the summer. It is best grown in an open, sunny position, but where there is a danger of cold, desiccating winter winds it should be given the protection of a south-facing wall. Within ten years it will have become an attractive evergreen of about 2m (6½ft) tall by 150cm (5ft) across and will thrive in any fertile garden soil. Avoid overfeeding it, though, or it will produce too much soft growth. If it becomes congested or unshapely prune and thin in June.

 4–5 ○ ◆

Crataegus oxyacantha

'Paul's Scarlet'

The **Midland Hawthorns** are less spiny than the common hawthorn and form attractive, small, round-headed trees. The handsome double flowered 'Paul's Scarlet' (sometimes offered as 'Coccinea Plena') is a great favourite in small gardens where its full height of about 6m (20ft) and spread of 3m (10ft) causes few problems of overcrowding or shading. The white cultivar 'Alba Plena' is similar in size but its flowers slowly turn pink as they mature. They are easy to grow in any good garden soil and, being particularly hardy and disease/pollution-resistant, make excellent specimens in a wide variety of situations.

 4–5 ◑ ◆

SPRING

Crinodendron hookerianum

C.hookerianum

The Chilean **Lantern Tree** is a disappointing plant in cold areas but in the milder parts of south and west England or where given the protection of a north- or east-facing wall, the sight of this shrub with its branches thickly hung with crimson, urn-shaped flowers among the evergreen foliage is astonishing and exotic. It flowers in May and demands lime-free soil and partial shade. In the right locality it will grow as high as 8m (26ft) with a spread of 4m (13ft) but is usually much smaller especially when grown against a wall in less mild areas. Any dead shoots or branches should be pruned out in January.

 5

Crocus chrysanthus

'E.A. Bowles'

There are a number of cultivars of *C.chrysanthus* available and all make excellent, free-flowering bulbs for naturalizing. They should be planted in groups at about 5cm (2in) deep with the corms 3cm (1¼ in) apart in an open, well-drained, sunny position and will soon multiply themselves. The deep, butter-yellow 'E.A.Bowles' is a long-established favourite and the striking mauve and white 'Lady Killer' makes a handsome contrast. 'Cream Beauty' and 'Blue Pearl' are ideal cultivars for those seeking softer colour-tones. All stand about 8cm (3in) tall and appreciate a liquid feed after flowering. When grown in a lawn, mow round them until the foliage has died away.

 3–4

Crocus vernus

'Queen of the Blues'

'Yellow Giant'

The large Dutch garden hybrids descended from the Alpine meadow crocus outshine their parent in every way. They are more vigorous in growth and their flowers are larger. They thrive in sunny, well-drained soils and are often seen in April and May flowering in great drifts in the lawns of parks and country houses. Never plant a mixture, always choose one particular colour for a particular spot and plant a bold clump of fifty or 100 corms 8cm (3in) deep and 5cm (2in) apart. The soft lilac-coloured 'Vanguard' is earlier than most, followed by the slightly darker 'Queen of the Blues'; 'Yellow Giant' is also quite early and the deep, wine-purple 'The Bishop' is very popular.

4–5 ○ ●●

Daphne odora

'Aureomarginata'

At the very beginning of spring this delightful dwarf shrub opens its clusters of deep pink buds to show attractive, white-tipped, sweetly fragrant flowers with reddish-purple centres. Even after ten years it will still be only a little over 100cm (3¼ ft) high and 150cm (5ft) across and only the variegated form 'Aureomarginata' will make much more growth than that. While the plant can withstand quite severe frosts it is often badly damaged by north or east winds and should be planted within the shelter of a building or other shrubs. It will thrive in any fertile soil provided it has a cool, moist root-run. Summer drought can be fatal.

2–3 ◑ ●●

SPRING

Dicentra eximia

D.eximia

Fringed Bleeding Heart is a graceful, cerise flowered perennial. An attractive plant for sun or partial shade, its long flowering period which usually commences in April and continues through to June makes it especially valuable in the herbaceous border. It usually grows to about 20cm (8in) tall but 'Spring Morning' and 'Alba' can grow as high as 50cm (20in). One plant would have a spread of about 30cm (12in) but if you divide and replant in March before flowering, you can soon establish a much larger patch. They demand that difficult combination of moist but well-drained soil, so incorporate plenty of peat and compost before planting.

 4–5 ◑ 🌢🌢🌢

Dodecatheon meadia

D.meadia

The **Shooting Star** is an intriguing plant for a moist, semi-shaded position. Its ground-hugging rosettes of foliage can be as much as 30cm (12in) across and the graceful flower stems emerging from the centre of the rosette in May and June are usually about 30cm (12in) tall. The clusters of rosy-purple flowers turn their petals back and point their bright yellow centres to the ground in exactly the same manner as cyclamen and they do indeed resemble shooting stars. The clumps can be increased by dividing and replanting in late September or October. The white form 'Album' is sometimes obtainable and is a very elegant and attractive plant.

 5–6 ◑ 🌢🌢🌢

SPRING

Epimedium

E. × warleyense

There are several species of **Barrenwort** available and all require similar growing conditions and perform the same useful function of providing attractive ground cover in shady or semi-shaded areas, especially among shrubs and trees. Although an herbaceous perennial, it retains its attractive bronze-red autumn foliage throughout the winter until it gives way to the new crown or heart-shaped leaves in the spring. *Epimedium versicolor* 'Sulphureum' is an attractive species with flowers the colour of old ivory. *E.macranthum* has bright green foliage and pale pink flowers while *E.× warleyense* has coppery-orange flowers. All bloom in April and May and are tolerant of any soil type.

🌺 4–5 ● ♦♦

Erythronium dens-canis and Erythronium tuolumnense

E.tuolumnense

E.dens-canis 'Lilac Wonder'

These graceful plants grow best in any moist, semi-shaded soil that includes a fair amount of humus. *E.dens-canis*, the **Dog's-Tooth Violet**, varies in colour from white or shell-pink to a rich crimson-purple. Most of the names such as 'Purple King', 'Rose Beauty', 'Snowflake' and 'Lilac Wonder' are self-explanatory. All grow to about 12cm (5in) tall and flower in April. Corms should be planted about 6cm (2¼ in) deep and clumps should be lifted and divided every fourth year. *E.tuolumnense* 'Pagoda' is a hybrid about 25cm (10in) tall with sulphur-yellow flowers.

🌺 4 ● ♦♦

SPRING

Eucalyptus gunnii

The **Cider Gum** is one of the hardiest of its genus and if allowed to do so will grow into an evergreen tree some 20m (66ft) tall with a spread of 12m (40ft) with perpetually peeling cinnamon-brown bark. It grows very rapidly and will attain almost two-thirds of its ultimate height and spread within twelve years. In most gardens, however, it is grown for its juvenile foliage and is therefore kept coppiced into a medium-sized shrub, say 3m (10ft) tall by 2m (6½ft) across. As the sprays of new silver-blue leaves develop in spring and early summer the branches bearing the older, olive-green foliage are pruned away right back to the base.

E.gunnii

Euphorbia griffithii 'Fireglow'

Most hardy, herbaceous **Euphorbias** are striking plants with heads of lime-green or yellow flowers but this cultivar has an extra trick: it surrounds each of its butter-yellow flowers with a brilliant flame-coloured bract giving the plant the appearance of bearing scarlet and gold flowers. In May and June the 45cm (18in) tall clumps are very useful in providing early colour in the herbaceous border. Any free-draining soil will suit them and they will do equally well in sun or semi-shade. Large clumps can be divided in early autumn but avoid getting the sap on your hands or in your eyes since it can cause severe irritation.

'Fireglow'

 5–6

59

SPRING

Exochorda × *macrantha* 'The Bride'

This attractive hybrid between
E.korolkowii and *E.racemosa* is
aptly nicknamed the **Pearl Bush**.
It is a vigorous plant and will
quite quickly make a large,
rather loose shrub some 3m
(10ft) tall by 2.5m (8ft) across.
The long arching sprays of pure
white flowers open in May.
Although it is tolerant of most
fertile, well-drained soils, on
shallow chalky ones the foliage
will become yellowed and sickly
and the plant will not thrive. If
pruning is required to keep the
shrub shapely then do it
immediately after flowering but
otherwise leave well alone
except to prune out dead wood
in March.

'The Bride'

 5

Forsythia × *intermedia* and *Forsythia suspensa*

Forsythia suspensa is a
marvellous species for growing
against a wall and does not
mind which way it faces. It can
attain a height of as much as 5m
(16ft) and a width of 4m (13ft)
after ten or twelve years, and the
long, trailing, golden sprays of
blossom look magnificent in
March. *F. × intermedia* is a
vigorous free-standing shrub up
to 2m (6½ft) tall and 2m in
diameter. The dwarf-growing
'Minigold' is perfect for smaller
gardens. All thrive in any garden
soil and grow equally well in sun
or semi-shade. In May prune out
all the sprays that have borne
flowers except those branches
required to extend the spread of
the plant.

F. x *intermedia* 'Spectabilis'

 3

SPRING

Fritillaria imperialis

F.imperialis

Their 60cm (24in) tall stems with nodding yellow or orange flowers and coronet of bright green leaves make the **Crown Imperial** one of the most exotic-looking plants in the border in April. Plant the bulbs on their sides about 15cm (6in) deep in a sunny, well-drained spot. If you need to divide the clumps later on wait until the bulbs have become dormant in mid-summer and transfer them straight to the new planting position being careful not to damage the bulb or you will be treated to a singularly unpleasant smell. A mulch of well-rotted compost every other spring will ensure a long and productive life.

 4 ▲▲▲

Fritillaria meleagris

F.meleagris

The **Snake's Head Lily** can still be found growing wild in some parts of Britain, but resist the temptation to dig it up or pick the flowers. Bulbs are freely available from a wide number of sources. Plant in clumps in a semi-shaded patch of rich, moist soil. Their 30cm (12in) tall stems bearing purple, pink or white chequered, bell-shaped flowers look especially attractive in a patch of rough grass or on the shadier side of a rock garden. The bulbs should be planted about 9cm (3½ in) deep and 5cm (2in) apart in groups of five or ten and clumps should be lifted and divided every fourth or fifth year in August.

 4 ▲▲▲

SPRING

Gentiana acaulis and Gentiana verna

G.verna

As a general rule the spring- and summer-flowering **Gentians** prefer open sunny sites with plenty of sunshine, while the autumn-flowering ones prefer a moist position in light shade. The other difference is that the spring and summer gentians demand the presence of lime in the soil while the autumn-flowering species hate it. The vivid blue trumpets of *G.acaulis* make pools of brilliant colour in late May while *G.verna* (**Spring Gentian**) is usually a slightly softer shade of blue and emerges in April. Both look particularly well at the edge of a path or tumbling over a large piece of rock. *G.verna* is also very attractive when planted between paving stones.

 4–5 ○ ◗

Geranium macrorrhizum

G.macrorrhizum

The hardy **Crane's Bills** are a very diverse family of herbaceous perennials and should never be confused with the half-hardy pelargoniums so frequently called geraniums by those who should know better. *G.macrorrhizum* is one of the earliest species to flower, often beginning in April if the spring has been mild. The 30cm (12in) dome of foliage is surmounted by a mass of rosy-pink flowers for several weeks. The large flowered 'Walter Ingwersen' is a softer pink than the type and there is a white form usually offered as 'Album'. They thrive in sun or light shade and are quite unfussy as to soil type so long as it is well drained.

 4–5 ◐ ◗

SPRING

Helleborus orientalis

H.orientalis

The **Lenten Rose** is much more variable than its cousin the Christmas rose and can be found in every shade from greeny-white through rose-pink to deepest mahogany-purple. It enjoys a shaded spot in free-draining soil which has been treated to a good helping of well-rotted compost, manure or leafmould before planting. An occasional top dressing of compost or leafmould is all that is required to keep it flourishing. The arching 30cm (12in) high sprays of glossy evergreen foliage are very handsome and the saucer-shaped flowers last and last, but resist the temptation to pick them because it is very difficult to make them survive more than twenty-four hours in a vase.

 3 ● ▲▲▲

Hepatica triloba

H.triloba

This attractive perennial may sometimes be labelled *H.nobilis* or even *Anemone hepatica*. From March to late April its star-shaped flowers stand out strongly against the dark green foliage. Most plants have sky-blue flowers but there are white, pink and red forms although these are seldom offered commercially. A mature clump will be about 30cm (12in) across and in flower will stand 9cm (3½in) high. Being a woodland plant it prefers semi-shaded places with cool, moist soils and an autumn mulch of leafmould is much appreciated. If you wish to spread the plant, lift and divide the clump in September but it needs a year or so to settle afterwards.

 3–4 ● ▲▲▲

SPRING

Hyacinthus orientalis

H.orientalis

The sweet scent from a bed of **Dutch Hyacinths** is very pleasing. They come in all shades of pink, blue, white and yellow. Don't go for the very large bulbs offered for forcing indoors as they will be very disappointing in succeeding years. Medium-sized bulbs planted about 5cm (2in) deep in a sunny, well-drained position will make a very effective display in April. Always try to incorporate some well-rotted or composted manure when planting. In summer when the bulbs have ripened and the foliage died down, lift them and store in a cool place in dry peat until planting out again the following February with a new dose of manure worked into the soil.

Iberis sempervirens

I.sempervirens

The **Perennial Candytuft** forms a 20cm (8in) high mound anything up to 150cm (5ft) across making it unsuitable for all but the largest rock garden, but it does look very handsome spilling over a retaining wall or at the edge of a path. The white flowers in May make the plant resemble a snowdrift for weeks on end and the dark, evergreen foliage is excellent weed-suppressing ground cover. In a dry, sunny position it can be left entirely to its own devices except for being dead-headed with shears or a strimmer immediately after flowering. The old cottage garden cultivar 'Snowflake' is still enormously popular but the more compact 'Little Gem' is better where space is limited.

SPRING

Ipheion uniflorum

'Album'

In April and May clumps of the **Spring Starflower** make a pleasing feature at the front of a border or a rock garden. Given a well-drained spot in full sun it will multiply itself rapidly and is perfectly at home in any type of soil. The clumps of grass-like foliage and the flower stems with their nodding heads of blue or white flowers stand about 15cm (6in) high. The bulbs should be lifted, separated and replanted every third autumn otherwise the clumps become congested and cease to flower. 'Wisley Blue' is a particularly good cultivar with sky-blue flowers. The deep violet 'Froyle Mill' and the white 'Album' are more difficult to obtain but well worth searching for.

 4 ○

Lamium maculatum

'Aureum'

The **Spotted Dead Nettle** is a very useful plant for poor soils in partial shade. Its green and silver foliage forms a very attractive, 10cm (4in) thick, weed-suppressing ground cover all year round and the pinkish-purple spikes of flowers bloom from April through to June. 'Beacon Silver' has particularly striking foliage but should be used only where its invasive habit will not become a nuisance. The golden-leafed 'Aureum' has very showy foliage but is not so tolerant of drought. It is often preferred, though, because it is less vigorous and can therefore be used in smaller gardens.

 4–6

SPRING

Leucojum vernum

L. vernum

In a moist, shaded spot between shrubs or under deciduous trees, clumps of **Spring Snowflake** make a pleasing feature in early March. At first glance the flowers seem to resemble those of the snowdrop and the plant does in fact demand the same kind of treatment. Dry bulbs are best planted in late summer, setting them about 10cm (4in) deep and 10cm apart. If purchased in the green they must be planted at once in their permanent position. They resent being disturbed but eventually you will find the clumps of flowers and foliage, about 20cm (8in) tall, produced every spring and increasing steadily.

🌷 3–4 ● ◗ ◗

Lysichitum americanum and *Lysichitum camtschatcense*

L. americanum

If planted in a boggy position in sun or semi-shade, *L. americanum* will put up spectacular displays of 40cm (16in) tall, golden-yellow flower spathes lasting from March to May. The long, brilliant green leaves develop after the flower and cover the ground with lush foliage for most of the summer. In the Japanese species, *L. camtschatcense*, the white flower spathes are seldom more than 15cm (6in) high and the leaves usually about 40cm (16in) long but otherwise it is similar in habit to its American cousin. Both can be propagated by dividing the developing clumps in early spring before they flower. Their peculiar smell has earned them the nickname **Skunk Cabbage**.

L. camtschatcense   🌷 3–5 ◑ ◗◗◗

SPRING

Magnolia stellata

M.stellata

This dainty species is slow growing and compact. Even when mature it will form a shrub of only 3m (10ft) high by 4m (13ft) across. The grey, furry flower buds on the bare winter branches hold a promise of spring which is more than fulfilled when the sweet-smelling, many-petalled white flowers open in their hundreds in March and April. It is reasonably lime-tolerant and will grow readily in a sunny or lightly shaded position. It flowers much earlier in life than its elegant cousin *M.kobus*. 'Water Lily' and 'Royal Star' are particularly good cultivars: they welcome shelter from cold winds in spring and appreciate a mulch of leafmould each autumn.

 3–4 ◐ ●●

Muscari armeniacum

M.armeniacum

Grape Hyacinths are a familiar sight in many gardens in March. They flourish in partial shade and establish easily in any soil, in fact they can become a bit of a menace, competing with other less vigorous bulbs and rock garden plants so it is inadvisable to mix them with plants that might later be swamped. The 18cm (7in) tall spikes of cobalt-blue flowers look most attractive at the edge of a border or among shrubs. The white species *M.botryoides* 'Album' is slightly smaller but equally pretty while the two-tone species *M.tubergenianum* is an attractive curiosity with half the flowers light blue and the rest dark blue, earning it the nickname **Oxford and Cambridge**.

M.tubergenianum 3 ● ●●

SPRING

Narcissus

'King Alfred'

'Peeping Tom'

'Suzy'

The genus *Narcissus* includes not only all the small delicate species and hybrids usually called by that name but also the larger flowered hybrids commonly called **Daffodils.** For exhibition purposes the genus is split into divisions.

From Division 1 the large pure white blooms of 'Mount Hood' have long been a garden feature and it is also a superb bulb for forcing — its 45cm (18in) stems allow it to be placed towards the back of a border where it can still be easily seen. The rich golden-yellow 'King Alfred' is also enormously popular. Bicolours such as 'Magnet' and 'Spring Glory' with their white perianths and golden trumpets are widely planted. In Division 2 flowers with red colouring in the cup such as 'Carbineer' and 'Fortune' are very good plants and the white and gold 'Tudor Minstrel' is equally vigorous. Division 3 includes plants which most people dub narcissi, such as the orange-yellow 'Jezebel' with a bright red cup or the white-petalled, red-cupped 'Verger'. These will naturalize readily in rough grass or in a sunny position among shrubs and are happy in any reasonably fertile well-drained soil. A liquid feed will help in poor soils and snipping the dead flowerhead off before it makes a seedpod is also beneficial. The double flowered cultivars of Division 4 such as the King Alfred sport 'Golden Ducat' and the yellow and orange 'Texas' are much appreciated as flowers for cutting and grow to a size similar to those in the first three divisions, but they look better growing in clumps in a border rather than being naturalized in

'Cheerfulness'

'Actea'

drifts. The dainty multi-headed stems of the Triandrus Narcissi of Division 5 grow to about 18cm (7in) tall and the deep yellow 'Liberty Bells' or milk-white 'Angels Tears' look delightful on a rock garden. Of the Cyclamineus Hybrid in Division 6 with their back-swept petals and early flowering date, 'Peeping Tom' is probably the most commonly offered but 'Dove Wings' and 'Charity May' are equally good. All grow to about 30cm (12in) tall and can either be naturalized in a sunny patch on the lawn or planted at the front of the border. The **Jonquil** Narcissi of Division 7 produce some of the sweetest-smelling blooms of the whole genus and the creamy-yellow 'Trevithian' or the primrose and orange 'Suzy' are especially fine cultivars. Division 8, the Tazetta Narcissi, includes the gorgeous double flowered 'Cheerfulness'. Poeticus Narcissi of Division 9 are most frequently represented by the orange-centred 'Pheasant Eye' but this old hybrid has to some extent been surpassed by 'Actea'. Since the former flowers in late May while the other is out in mid-April there is no reason why they shouldn't both be planted. The split corona cultivars of Division 10 such as 'Frileuse' or 'Parisienne' look well in the strict formal setting of a patio island bed. Most of the species of Division 11 are miniatures and best suited to the rock garden. N.bulbocodium with its bell-shaped flowers on 8cm (3in) stems and the dainty 6cm (2¼ in) tall N.juncifolius are especially lovely.

N.bulbocodium 2–5 ○

SPRING

Omphalodes cappadocica

O.cappadocica

This pretty little perennial rejoices in the name **Navelwort**. It is an excellent plant for ground cover in moist shady or semi-shaded areas and four plants set in a square 40cm (16in) apart from each other will soon join up to make a weed-smothering mat some 15cm (6in) high and over 100cm (3¼ ft) across. The delicate china-blue flowers are borne in stiff sprays above the foliage and usually bloom throughout April and May. Another closely related species is *O.verna*, also known as **Blue Eyed Mary**, which is slightly larger and more vigorous and even more shade-tolerant, but one does not come across it so often in nurseries or garden centres.

Ornithogalum nutans and *Ornithogalum umbellatum*

O.nutans

These hardy bulbous plants naturalize readily in a moist, semi-shaded spot at the edge of a border or shrubbery. *O.nutans* stands about 30cm (12in) tall with drooping, bell-shaped flowers that have a broad, jade-green stripe running down the back of each petal. They are natives of southern Europe and larger than the indigenous British species *O.umbellatum* which is often known in cottage gardens as the **Star of Bethlehem**. This species is slightly later flowering, stands only 12cm (5½ in) tall and sometimes spreads itself so freely that it becomes a nuisance. In both cases the bulbs should be planted about 6cm (2¼ in) deep and not disturbed thereafter.

O.umbellatum 3–4

SPRING

Picea abies 'Little Gem'

P.abies 'Little Gem'

Among the slow-growing dwarf conifers this delightful compact little plant thoroughly deserves its name. Planted in an open, sunny, well-drained spot on a rock garden or at the edge of a low retaining wall it will form a dense dome of fresh green foliage which, even after ten years, will still stand only 30cm (12in) high and about 40cm (16in) across. Like some others of its genus, the new shoots that begin to unfold in spring are a brilliant lime green and very striking and remain until well into the summer. It associates well with other dwarf shrubs such as rhododendron 'Chikor' or hebe 'Quicksilver'.

○ ♦♦

Pieris japonica

'Purity'

'Mountain Fire'

There are numerous forms of P.japonica, all excellent shrubs for a semi-shaded position in lime-free soil. The glossy foliage is handsome at any time of year but in late spring, as the long panicles of white or pink flower buds open, their effect is complemented by the unfolding of the coppery-coloured foliage of the new season's growth which slowly turns green as the summer progresses. 'Purity' is an attractive Japanese-raised seedling whose snow-white flowers are somewhat larger than most and 'Mountain Fire' has particularly striking wine-coloured new foliage each year. After ten years the shrub will probably stand about 2m (6½ft) tall and 2m across although the variegated form 'Variegata' may attain only half that.

 4 ● ♦♦♦

SPRING

Polygonatum multiflorum

P.multiflorum

Solomon's Seal is a striking woodland perennial which adapts readily to a shaded or partially shaded corner in any fertile soil. The long arching fronds of foliage form a shuttlecock-shaped clump with the small greenish-white flowers strung along the underside of the mid-ribs like pearl drops. If too well fed the plant can become invasive but in association with such vigorous companions as crocosmia, hellebores or ferns it will make a graceful contribution in areas beneath large trees or at the foot of a north- or west-facing wall. By dividing the clumps every third autumn and replanting only a portion, you can keep the plant in bounds.

Primula denticulata

P.denticulata

The 30cm (12in) tall heads of white or mauve flowers of this attractive March-flowering **Primula** usually begin to open before the foliage is fully developed. They often bloom for a month or more and are probably the easiest of garden primulas to grow. They succeed in any moist garden soil in sun or partial shade. Most plants offered are grown from seed so the flowers can be anything from pale lilac to deep mauve, or wine-coloured or even white. Named forms such as 'Bressingham Beauty' and 'Alba' are propagated by division in autumn and their colour is therefore guaranteed — so if you see one that particularly takes your fancy, find out first where it came from.

SPRING

Primula japonica

P. japonica

This graceful waterside perennial with its 45cm (18in) tall stems bearing tiers of flowers is one of the group known as **Candelabra Primulas**. They thrive in moist or boggy soils in a semi-shaded position and look especially effective at the margin of a stream or pond. The flowers are usually reddish purple but there is a white form 'Postford White' and also a brilliant red one called 'Miller's Crimson'. Once established they will often produce self-sown seedlings which can be easily transplanted when young, but the parent plants should not be disturbed once they have established themselves.

🌷 4–5 ◑ 💧💧💧

Primula veris and Primula vulgaris

P. vulgaris 'Wanda'

The **Cowslip** and the **Common Primrose** are part of Britain's natural heritage and if you want them in your garden there is absolutely no need to dig them out of the hedgerows. Both are easily grown from seed or commercially obtainable as growing plants. Both grow best in heavy, moist fertile soil in a semi-shaded position. Primula vulgaris has given rise to a number of attractive colour forms as well as the usual soft yellow, and these are fairly widely available. 'Wanda' is a rich wine-purple flower and 'Blue Riband' a handsome royal blue. The recently discovered pale pink form is now being offered commercially by a few sources as 'Sue Jervis'.

🌷 3–4 ◑ 💧💧💧

SPRING

Prunus laurocerasus

P.laurocerasus

The **Cherry Laurel** is widely used as an evergreen screening shrub against wind, noise and traffic fumes. It tolerates shade and drips from overhanging trees and grows vigorously on all soils except shallow chalky ones. Left to itself it could make a shrub more than 5m (16ft) tall and 5m across but an annual prune will keep it well within bounds. Two interesting forms which are good ornamental shrubs in their own right are 'Otto Luyken', which seldom attains more than 2m (6½ft) in height and a spread of about 100cm (3¼ft) and flowers freely in April; and 'Zabeliana' which is equally low growing and free flowering but with attractive narrow foliage.

 4

Prunus serrulata

'Tai-Haku'

'Kiku-shidare Sakara'

The hybrid **Japanese Cherries** are usually catalogued under *P.serrulata* although it is more than probable that other species have contributed to their pedigree somewhere along the line. They thrive in any well-drained garden soil and look their best in a sunny position. Most are small, round-headed trees standing about 5m (16ft) tall when mature although the white 'Tai-Haku' will grow as tall as 7m (22½ft). The upright 'Ama-no-Gawa' (sometimes offered as 'Erecta') has a very narrow silhouette, seldom more than 100cm (3¼ft) across, while 'Kiku-shidare Sakura' is a graceful weeping form (sometimes offered erroneously as 'Cheals Weeping Cherry').

 4

74

SPRING

Pulmonaria saccharata

'Pink Dawn'

This species of **Lungwort** offers a wide choice of forms, all of which make excellent ground cover for shady corners. They are tolerant of all soils and spread themselves with considerable vigour so avoid putting them alongside plants that can't stand up to aggressive competition. The flowers can be white, pink or blue and are borne in April and May above foliage attractively marbled with white or silver. They usually stand between 25cm and 30cm (10—12in) high. 'Argentea' and 'Pink Dawn' are much valued for their foliage. One of the most invasive forms is 'Bowles Red', while 'Highdown' opens its dark blue flowers earlier than most of the others.

 4—5 ● ◆◆

Pulsatilla vulgaris

P. vulgaris

The **Pasque Flower** is occasionally offered as *Anemone pulsatilla*. It requires a sunny, well-drained position and is happiest on chalky soils, so if your garden soil is acid give it a dusting of lime when planting and an occasional top dressing. The star-shaped, violet-purple flowers emerge before the foliage has developed. The clumps are usually about 15cm (6in) tall and can be as much as 30cm (12in) across when established. Red and white flowered forms are also available and seed taken from these usually yields a high proportion of seedlings that are the same colour as their parent.

 3—4 ○ ◆◆

SPRING

Pyrethrum

'Brenda'

'Elaine May Robinson'

The garden hybrid **Pyrethrums** derived from *P.roseum* are among the earliest of the mainstream border perennials to flower. In May and early June their daisy-like flowers in varying shades of pink help carry over from the last of the spring bulbs to the main blaze of summer colour. The yellow-centred, shocking-pink 'Brenda' and the soft, rose-pink 'Elaine May Robinson' are popular cultivars and the shell-pink double flowered 'Vanessa' is also very attractive although sometimes harder to obtain. They succeed best in a sunny position on any light, well-drained soil and the clumps can be divided every fourth year immediately after flowering.

Rhododendron 'Blue Tit', 'Elizabeth' and 'Chikor'

'Blue Tit'

Not all **Rhododendrons** are fit only for very large gardens. These three are all dwarf in habit and excellent plants for moist, semi-shaded sites in any garden where there is no trace of lime in the soil. 'Blue Tit' will form a dense shrub up to 100cm (3¼ ft) high and 100cm across over a period of twelve to fifteen years. Its lavender-blue flowers darken as they grow older. 'Elizabeth' is a very popular cultivar with bright scarlet flowers and will attain a height of about 60cm (24in) by about 80cm (33in) across within ten years. 'Chikor' has warm, butter-yellow flowers and grows only 20cm (8in) tall and 25cm (10in) across.

SPRING

Rhododendron yakushimanum

R. yakushimanum

This species was only discovered this century and introduced from Japan to the UK in 1934. It forms a compact bush up to 130cm (4½ ft) tall and the same in width. It has already proved an excellent garden plant and has produced a wide range of hybrids, most of which are similar to their parent in size but differ widely in flower colour. A group raised and introduced by Waterers nursery were named after the Seven Dwarfs, 'Bashful', 'Doc', 'Dopey', and so on. Like all rhododendrons they demand moist, lime-free soil and partial shade, and this particular group make excellent tub plants for balconies or roof gardens as well.

 5 ● ▲▲▲

Rhododendron **Hardy Hybrids**

'Pink Pearl'

Most of these will form substantial shrubs of 2m or 3m (6½ –10ft) high by 1.5m to 2m (5 – 6½ ft) across although some do grow smaller. Colours range from the pale flesh-coloured 'Pink Pearl' and the clear white 'Mum' to the cobalt-coloured 'Blue Peter' or the brilliant scarlet-crimson 'Britannia'. They require moist, lime-free soil and partial shade. They also resent being restricted, so there is no point in trying to shoe-horn them into a confined space with the intention of keeping them pruned small — they simply won't perform. Being dense and evergreen they are well worth considering as an informal hedge or screen.

 4–5 ● ▲▲▲

SPRING

Salix helvetica

S.helvetica

This attractive shrubby **Willow** is a very good choice for smaller gardens. Even when fully grown it will rarely be higher than 150cm (5ft) and would not spread more than 100cm (3¼ ft) across. In spring the young stems, leaves and catkins are covered in soft grey fur. It will grow equally well in sun or shade and is completely unfussy as to soil type. Prolonged summer drought, however, can cause the plant some distress and may make it drop its foliage early, but unless conditions are very severe it should recover the following season. It associates well with summer-flowering shrubs such as hibiscus or kalmia.

Scilla campanulata

The **Spanish Bluebell** is usually the last of the scillas to flower and is another of those unfortunate plants with several names. You may see it offered as *Endymion hispanicus* or as *Scilla hispanica*. Whatever it's properly called, it is a most attractive garden plant. The 40cm (16in) tall stems with their spikes of bell-shaped flowers emerging from the dense rosette of long flat leaves look delightful in semi-shaded corners. The bulbs should be planted 8cm (3in) deep and 8cm apart and once established will multiply themselves with gusto. There are pink, blue and white forms and all appreciate a mulch of leafmould in the autumn if it is available.

S.campanulata

SPRING

Skimmia japonica

'Rubella'

This pollution-proof, shade-tolerant evergreen is a highly adaptable shrub. It is equally at home in acid or alkaline soils and forms a slow-growing bush which will attain a height of 150cm (5ft) and a spread of 120cm (4ft) after about ten years. The clusters of white flowers appear in April and May but this is one of those plants where male flowers appear on one bush while female flowers grow on another, and if you want the brilliant scarlet berries that follow the female flowers you will have to grow a male alongside. 'Rubella' is a good male clone with sweetly scented flowers and 'Foremanii' is a very free-fruiting female clone.

 4–5

Spiraea × arguta

S. x arguta

This attractive hybrid between S.multiflora and S.thunbergii is usually called the **Bridal Wreath**. In April and May the long graceful, arching branches are weighed down with a froth of pure white blossom. It is happy in any garden soil and grows equally well in sun or partial shade. Since the flowers are borne on one-year-old wood the shrub must be pruned as soon as it has finished flowering: remove all those sprays which have borne flowers and allow the new growth to develop and ripen. The fresh, bright green foliage forms an attractive background for later-flowering perennials making it a good choice as a specimen shrub for the back of a border.

 4–5

SPRING

Syringa vulgaris

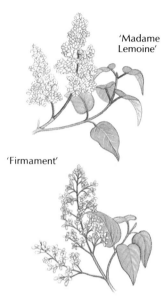

'Madame Lemoine'

'Firmament'

The **Common Lilac** is one of the most elegant, sweetly scented shrubs available to gardeners. There are an enormous number of named cultivars and their flowering period varies from mid-May to early June. As well as the familiar blue and white shades there are also pink, purple and yellow flowered plants. The white, double flowered 'Madame Lemoine' was introduced about 1890 and is still a firm favourite and the clear lilac-blue 'Firmament' raised by the same nursery some forty years later is equally popular. They grow well in any soil but are particularly suited to chalky ones. A site in full sun is best for them although they will tolerate light shade.

🌼 5–6   ◐   🌢

Thymnus 'Anderson's Gold'

'Anderson's Gold'

This dwarf **Thyme** forms a spreading mat about 3cm (1¼ in) high and when mature will be about 60cm (24in) across. For most of the year its foliage is a greenish-yellow but in late winter it turns a brilliant gold which makes it stand out all spring like a patch of sunshine, even on the dullest day. It looks very attractive in a sunny, well-drained spot on a rock garden or at the edge of a path. It could even be planted between the paving stones. If you have a hot dry area which is unsuccessful as a lawn then a large patch of prostrate thyme is a very acceptable alternative with the added virtues of no mowing and no summer watering.

🌼 5   ○   🌢

SPRING

Trillium grandiflorum and *Trillium sessile*

T.grandiflorum

T.sessile

The **Wake Robin** — *Trillium grandiflorum* — and its cousin *Trillium sessile* are attractive woodland plants from North America. They are happiest in moist, well-drained, peaty soil in semi-shade. *T.grandiflorum* stands about 45cm (18in) tall with large, pure white three-petalled flowers that gradually turn a warm rose colour as they age. *T.sessile* is only 20cm (8in) tall and its flowers are a rich maroon which is echoed in the dark purple blotches on its leaves. In both cases the bulbs should be planted as soon as they are received, about 8cm (3in) deep and 10cm (4in) apart, and you may find that they take a year or two to settle.

 4 ● ▲▲▲

Tulipa greigii and *Tulipa kaufmanniana*

T.greigii

T.kaufmanniana

These delightful dwarf **Tulips** are very undemanding. The bulbs should be planted in October about 10cm (4in) deep and 10cm apart in a sunny, well-drained spot. The foliage of the *greigii* hybrids is attractively marbled. The bright vermilion 'Royal Splendour' with his brother the yellow and red 'Oriental Splendour' are firm favourites. 'Heart's Delight' is probably the most popular *kaufmanniana* hybrid with its pale pink and dark red petals and the smaller-growing 'Gluck' is also a favourite. They should be dead-headed as soon as the petals have fallen and a liquid feed after flowering is also beneficial.

 3–4 ◑ ▲▲

SPRING

Tulipa praestans 'Fusilier'

This striking dwarf **Tulip** is probably the best of the multi-headed species available. Bulbs planted in October about 10cm (4in) deep and 15cm (6in) apart will send up one 20cm (8in) tall stem carrying up to five flower buds which open to the most brilliant, eye-catching orange-scarlet in mid-April. The colour is one best seen alone against a background of evergreen shrubs or at the foot of a wall — although it does seem to associate reasonably well with dark blue grape hyacinths. Like other tulips it succeeds best in a sunny, well-drained spot and has a preference for chalky soils but should not be disturbed once established.

'Fusilier'   🌸 4–5   ◑   ♦♦

Tulips: Darwin and New Darwin Hybrids

'Sweet Harmony'

'Gudoshnik'

Darwin Tulips generally stand up to 75cm (30in) tall and flower in mid-May. The bulbs should be planted in late autumn about 10cm (4in) deep and 20cm (8in) apart. 'Clara Butt', 'The Bishop' and 'Sweet Harmony' are established favourites. Crossing Darwin tulips with *T.greigii* and *T.fosteriana* has produced a race of new hybrids which flower about four weeks earlier, such as the yellow and scarlet 'Apeldoorn' and the peach and rose 'Gudoshnik'. All thrive in sunny, well-drained soil and are best lifted each year as soon as the foliage has died down or, alternatively, plant them 15cm (6in) deep and apply a heavy dressing of lime in late summer.

🌸 4–5   ○   ♦♦

SPRING

Tulips: Parrot Flower Hybrids

'Fantasy'

These exotic-looking **Tulips** bloom in mid-May. Some older hybrids had rather weak stems incapable of supporting the flower properly, but modern ones are more vigorous and larger flowered. In most cases the names, such as 'Black Parrot', 'Red Parrot' and 'White Parrot' are self-explanatory, but don't overlook 'Fantasy' with its deep salmon-pink petals fringed and crested with green and white. The bulbs should be planted in late autumn about 10cm (4in) deep and 15cm (6in) apart in a sunny, well-drained site. If they cannot be lifted in summer when the foliage has died down, give a good top dressing of lime, watering it in well.

  5 ○ ♦♦

Viburnum carlesii

This handsome medium-sized shrub has been enormously popular since its introduction from Korea at the beginning of this century. In early May the coral-pink buds open to form clusters of sweetly scented, pinkish-white flowers which perfume the air for yards around. The shrub is relatively slow growing, generally attaining a height of 150cm (5ft) and a spread of 150cm over ten years and rarely exceeding 2m by 2m (6½ by 6½ft) even when fully mature. Totally unfussy as to soil type, it prefers to be sited in semi-shade. The clone 'Aurora' is an outstanding form with pinker flowers than the original species.

'Aurora'

  5 ◑ ♦♦

SPRING

Vinca major

V.major

The **Greater Periwinkle** is an excellent trailing evergreen shrub for shaded or semi-shaded areas of the garden but it must be kept firmly under control. The flowering shoots stand up to 50cm (20in) high and since the plant's lateral shoots root themselves as they creep along the ground, the spread is whatever you allow it to be. It makes good cover for sloping banks or bare patches around or underneath shrubs and its bright blue flowers in April and May are most attractive. The variegated form is fractionally less vigorous than the plain leafed one. They tolerate any soil and are more drought-resistant than most woodland plants.

 4–5 ● ◗

Viola hederaceae and *Viola labradorica*

V.hederaceae

These two April-flowering **Violets** are quite different in character but both enjoy moist shaded sites and detest summer drought. *V.hederaceae* is a dainty, trailing perennial with fresh green foliage and tiny blue and white flowers. It appreciates a mulch of well-rotted leafmould in autumn. *V.labradorica* has bronzy-purple foliage which forms an attractive contrast to the pale lilac-blue flowers. While *V.hederaceae* is never more than 10cm (4in) high and spreading about 30cm (12in), *V.labradorica* will swiftly form a broad patch 15cm (6in) high and 100cm (3¼ ft) across smothering everything else that gets in its way.

V.labradorica

 4–5 ● ●●●

Waldsteinia ternata

This unusual, easy-going little rockery perennial is not always easy to obtain but well worth including in your collection. The light green leaves are visible all year round and in April are almost hidden beneath a mass of primrose-yellow flowers. It prefers cool, semi-shaded places but will tolerate full sun and is equally happy in acid or alkaline soils. In bloom, the plant is about 10cm (4in) high and an established specimen could be up to 40cm (16in) across. Its relatively non-invasive nature makes it a good choice as a companion for slow-growing saxifrages or dwarf tulips.

W.ternata

Wisteria floribunda and Wisteria sinensis

Wisteria is a glorious climber for a south- or west-facing wall or to send rambling through an old tree. The Japanese wisteria, _W.floribunda_, is widely planted, particularly the white and pink forms, and 'Macrobotrys' with its enormously elongated sprays of flowers, often as much as 100cm (3¼ ft) long, is much sought-after. The Chinese wisteria, _W.sinensis_, is often preferred because of its sweet scent and more floriferous habit. The plants must be carefully pruned each year, first in August to shorten the leafy shoots back to within 15cm (6in) of the main branch and again in late January, back to within three or four buds from the main branch. New specimens usually refuse to open their leaf buds until mid-summer in the first season.

W.floribunda

SUMMER

During this period the flower garden reaches the peak of its display. The brilliance and beauty of herbaceous plants and summer-flowering trees and shrubs transforms even the tiniest backyard or patio into a patch of heaven. The hard work and careful preparation of the previous autumn and spring is now magnificently rewarded and, if the groundwork has been well done, gardening can be taken relatively easily. Where plants have been positioned properly, their foliage will overlap and shade the ground, preventing the majority of weed seeds from germinating. Weeds such as bindweed should be controlled by painting the leaves with a translocated herbicide. A regular spraying of one of the proprietory insecticides mixed with a liquid fertilizer will prevent greenfly infestations and promote healthy new growth — this should be commenced in late spring as soon as the new foliage has started into growth. Never wait until the attack is established before taking action or you could well be too late. For roses, the three-in-one sprays that incorporate insecticide, fungicide and foliar feed make a huge difference to the plant's performance and usually need applying only once or twice a month.

Summer-flowering shrubs, such as *Weigela,* that produce their blooms on one-year-old wood must have the old-flowering growth pruned out as soon as they have finished flowering. Care must be taken of drought-sensitive plants if the season is a particularly dry one.

SUMMER

Acanthus mollis and Acanthus spinosus

A.mollis

A.spinosus

Both species of this statuesque perennial are commonly called **Bear's Breeches** but the reason for this appellation is lost. A.mollis is usually the taller of the two at 160cm (5¼ ft), although the form 'Latifolius' will grow only to about 110cm (3½ ft) tall. A.spinosus usually grows to about 120cm (4ft) tall and all have a spread of about 80cm (2¾ ft). A.mollis will tolerate partial shade but A.spinosus must have full sun and free-draining soil. New plants can be propagated by dividing the clumps in April but this may mean that the flowers in July and August will be less profuse for the first season after division.

 7–8 ◑ ◆

Achillea ptarmica 'The Pearl'

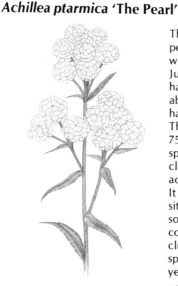

'The Pearl'

The **Sneezewort** is an excellent perennial. The clouds of small white flowers usually last from July to September and the handsome dark green foliage is absolutely weedproof once it has covered its appointed site. The plant usually stands about 75cm (30in) tall and with its spreading habit will form a clump up to 100cm (3¼ ft) across within four or five years. It prefers sunny, well-drained sites but has no preference for soil type. A spring mulch of compost is beneficial, and the clumps can be divided in spring every fourth or fifth year.

  6–10 ○ ◆

SUMMER

Aconitum napellus

'Bressingham Spire'

The **Monkshood**'s slightly sinister reputation arises from the fact that its roots are poisonous and its foliage and seeds are also slightly toxic. For all that, its imposing 100cm (3¼ ft) tall spikes of blue flowers above a clump of dark green foliage make it a popular perennial for the back of the border. It prefers moist soil and a semi-shaded position; an autumn mulch of leafmould as the foliage dies down is a good idea. Clumps can be divided in spring if they become too large. The violet-blue 'Bressingham Spire' is one of the most popular cultivars available, but the blue and white 'Blue Sceptre' and the dark 'Newry Blue' can still sometimes be found.

 8–10 ◑ ●●●

Actinidia chinensis and *Actinidia kolomikta*

A.chinensis

A.kolomikta

Both species make attractive climbers for a trellis on a south- or west-facing wall and thrive in any fertile garden soil. *A.chinensis*, the **Chinese Gooseberry**, will reach a height of 9m (30ft) and a spread of about 4m (13ft) within twelve years, and its huge, heart-shaped leaves and creamy-white August blossoms are very striking. The hairy brown fruits, also known as kiwi fruit, are produced only if both a male and a female plant are grown. *A.kolomikta* is rarely more than 6m (20ft) tall and 2m (6½ ft) across. Prune out dead wood or unwanted shoots in winter.

 8 ○ ●●

SUMMER

Agapanthus

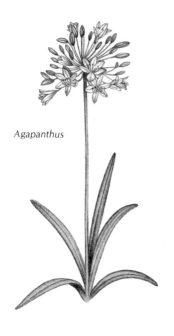

Agapanthus

The most reliably hardy plants of this attractive South African genus are derived from the 'Headbourne Hybrids'. Some named clones are offered: these include a white form, but most are shades of blue ranging from a light sky-blue to deepest violet. They require well-drained soil and full sun and usually bloom in August and September. The bulbs should be planted 15cm (6in) apart and protected each winter with a thick mulch of peat or leafmould. The flowers generally stand about 70cm (28in) tall and a well-established clump could be up to 80cm (2¾ft) across. If grown in tubs, the tubs should be moved into a cool shed or cellar for the winter.

 8–9 ○ ◊

Alchemilla mollis

A.mollis

The fan-shaped leaves of this delightful perennial make it easy to see why its common name is **Lady's Mantle**. It grows in any moist soil in sun or semi-shade and spreads itself readily by seed. The plant with its loose sprays of greenish-yellow flowers usually stands up to 45cm (18in) high with a spread of 40cm (16in). It is also a favourite because of its charming trick of balancing dewdrops or raindrops on its leaves like jewels in the morning sunshine. It makes good ground cover underneath rose bushes, hibiscus and similar shrubs.

 6–9 ◑ ◊

Allium aflatunense, Allium cernuum and Allium moly

A.aflatunense

A.cernuum

A.moly

These three species of ornamental onion are striking summer-flowering bulbs for a sunny, well-drained herbaceous border. They thrive equally well in acid or chalky soils and, once planted, require very little attention. *A.aflatunense* will send up an elegant stem about 75cm (30in) tall surmounted by a ball of rosy-purple flowers in late May or June. The bulbs should be planted about 10cm (4in) deep and 20cm (8in) apart as soon as they are obtained, which is usually in autumn or early winter. The **Nodding Onion**, *A.cernuum*, puts up a clump of narrow, strap-like leaves from which, in late July, emerges a 40cm (16in) stem bearing an attractive head of drooping purple flowers. Bulbs should be planted about 5cm (2in) deep in groups of five or ten with 10cm (4in) between bulbs. The **Golden Garlic**, *A.moly*, is an eye-catching plant for the rock garden or the edge of a border. It naturalizes readily and will tolerate light shade. The flowerheads in flat groups of brilliant golden-yellow stars appear in June and July and usually stand about 25cm (10in) tall above mounds of grey-green foliage. The bulbs should be planted as soon as they are received, in groups of ten or so 5cm (2in) deep and 10cm (4in) apart. Flowering will seem sparse in the first year or two, but you will soon have a fine clump. Divide in September about every five years.

5–7

SUMMER

Alstroemeria Ligtu Hybrids

Ligtu Hybrid

The gorgeously coloured
Peruvian Lily is often best
grown from seed with the one-
year-old seedling planted out
in May with minimal root
disturbance as deep as possible
in a sunny position. The soil
must have well-rotted manure
or compost dug in. If you buy
the fleshy tuber-like roots,
plant them at least 15cm (6in)
deep and don't worry when
nothing appears in the first
year. The pink, flame or orange
flowers usually begin in July,
standing some 90cm (3ft) tall
above a clump of foliage up to
80cm (2¾ft) across.

 7 ○ ◗◗

Anchusa azurea

'Loddon
Royalist'

This brilliant blue perennial is a
most valuable plant for the
herbaceous border. The 90cm
(3ft) tall clumps of gentian-blue
flowers are in evidence from
May to July and help bridge
the gap between spring-
flowering bulbs and the
mainstream summer-flowering
perennials. They are best
planted between November
and March in a sunny site in
well-drained soil. They are
quite unfussy as to soil type
and will soon establish a clump
some 60cm (24in) across. They
do not take kindly to being
divided or disturbed but a
spring dressing of general
purpose fertilizer is beneficial.
'Loddon Royalist' and the sky-
blue 'Opal' are popular.

6–8 ○ ◗

SUMMER

Anemone coronaria de Caen and St Brigid strains

St Brigid

de Caen

These two strains of the **Poppy Anemone** make a brilliant patch of colour at the front of a border. If you purchase a quantity of corms and plant a few at the beginning of each month from October to April, you will have a succession of flowers from March to the end of the summer; in following years they will gradually even themselves out to bloom in early summer. The St Brigid anemones are semi-double flowered while the de Caen are single, and both grow about 25cm (10in) tall. The tubers should be planted 5cm (2in) deep and 5cm apart in a sunny site, and they welcome a mulch of compost in autumn.

 6–7 ○ ◆

Astilbe × *arendsii*

'Deutschland'

'Fanal'

These handsome hybrids flourish in rich, moist soil in partial shade and must be kept well watered in the event of a dry summer. Their height can vary from 50cm (20in) to 100cm (3¼ ft) and the spread of an established plant is usually about 40cm (16in). The plumes of flowers are borne above the mound of dark green foliage from June to August and a handful of general purpose fertilizer in spring as the new shoots begin to emerge helps ensure a good summer display. Among the most popular cultivars are the rich red 'Fanal', the neat, cerise 'Düsseldorf' and the pure white 'Deutschland'.

 6–8 ● ◆◆◆

SUMMER

Astrantia

A.major 'Variegata'

All species and forms of **Masterwort** are good perennials for light shade and, provided there is plenty of moisture, they thrive equally well in acid or alkaline soils. The unusual toothed flowerheads vary from greenish-white to dark pink, and all generally begin to flower in June. A.major, A.involucrata and A.maxima all stand about 90cm (3ft) tall in flower and form a neat bushy mound of foliage some 60cm (24in) across, although the crimson flowered A.major 'Rubra' and the greenish-white 'Variegata' are usually smaller. Divide the clumps in March or October.

🌺 6–9　◐　💧💧💧

Azalea

'Gibraltar'

'Mother's Day'

Strictly speaking, these should be listed under Rhododendron but many commercial sources still treat them as if they were a separate genus. They require cool, moist, lime-free soils in semi-shade. There are both deciduous and evergreen hybrids available and, generally speaking, the evergreen ones flower in May while the deciduous ones give their dazzling displays in early June. Of the deciduous cultivars, the brilliant golden-orange 'Gibraltar' and salmon-pink 'Cecile' are deservedly popular among the hundreds of hybrids on offer, while of the evergreens the rich purple 'Velvet Gown' and the rosy-red 'Mother's Day' are among the most frequently planted.

🌺 4–5　●　💧💧💧

Berberidopsis corallina

B.corallina

The **Coral Plant** is a most interesting evergreen shrub to train against a north-facing or shaded west wall. Its two chief dislikes are lime in the soil and direct sunshine, and it can also be quite severely damaged by cold winter winds. In spite of being a bit on the delicate side, its leathery, dark green foliage and brilliant, deep crimson flowers in July and August make it a striking feature in any garden. Within ten years it could attain a height of as much as 5m (16ft) and a spread of 6m (20ft) if allowed. Prune in early spring to remove dead, weak or unwanted shoots.

 7–8

Berberis × *carminea*

'Barbarossa'

This colourful group of deciduous hybrids comprises vigorous spreading shrubs which vary from 1.5m to 2.5m (5 – 8ft) tall and spread up to 120cm (4ft) across. The bright yellow flowers are most attractive, but they also have brilliant autumn colouring and magnificent berries. 'Pirate King' is one of the more upright growing clones and has bright orange-red berries while 'Buccaneer' has larger berries which begin shell-pink and gradually turn deep red. They are happy in sun or semi-shade on any free-draining soil. If pruning is required, do it either after flowering in July or else in winter once the birds have taken the berries.

 7

SUMMER

Buddleia davidii

'Black Knight'

The **Butterfly Bush** grows well in a warm, sunny spot on any soil. The sweetly scented flowers bloom in July on the new season's growth, so the plant should be pruned back to the emerging shoots close to the base in early March. If pruned right back every year, the shrub will rarely grow more than 2m (6½ft) tall or spread more than 150cm (5ft), but if a couple of main stems are allowed to develop, the height and spread could eventually be three times that. The purple 'Black Knight' and the white 'Peace' are popular cultivars, and 'Harlequin' has variegated foliage.

  7 ◑ ♦

Calluna vulgaris

C. vulgaris

The **Common Moorland Heather** is often known as **Ling** in Scotland to distinguish it from Scotch or grey heather (*Erica cinerea*). All cultivars demand an open, sunny, well-drained site on lime-free soil. Their flowering period is August and September and the range of colours available is enormous. Their height can vary according to cultivar, so that the long-flowering, double pink 'H.E.Beale' at 60cm (24in) tall and 60cm across seems to bear little relation to the white 'Kinlochruel' at only 20cm (8in) tall and 30cm (12in) across. There are also golden-and-bronze-leafed forms. After flowering, the dead heads should be clipped off with shears.

   8–9 ○ ♦♦

Camassia

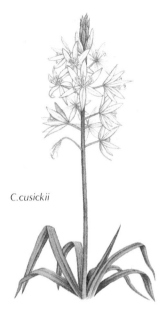

C.cusickii

The two species of **Bear Grass** most commonly offered are *C.cusickii* and *C.quamash* (sometimes offered as *C.esculenta*). Both thrive in sunny, well-drained positions and, once planted, the bulbs can be left undisturbed to multiply themselves, which they do freely after a few years. *C.quamash* is about 80cm (2¾ft) tall in bloom and the flowers are sometimes bright violet-blue, sometimes mauve. *C.cusickii* is pale lilac and shorter, usually only 50cm (20in) tall. The bulbs are surprisingly large and should be planted as soon as they are received, about 15cm (6in) deep and 20cm (8in) apart.

   6 ○ ●

Campanula

C.cochlearifolia

This enormous genus of herbaceous perennials and annuals includes plants of all shapes and sizes from ground-hugging alpines to the imposing *C.lactiflora* and *C.latifolia* which bloom at the back of so many herbaceous borders in July and August.

For the rock garden or at the front of a border in a sunny, well-drained position, *C.cochlearifolia* cultivars are a popular choice. None grows more than 10cm (4in) tall, forming a cushion 20cm (8in) across. The colours range from white to dark Oxford-blue and some named forms such as 'Blue Tit' and 'Alba' are obtainable.

C.carpatica hybrids such as 'Blue Moonlight', 'Chewton Joy'

SUMMER

C.glomerata
'Superba'

C. latifolia
'White Ladies'

and 'Bressingham White' make slightly larger clumps standing up to 25cm (10in) tall and about 20cm (8in) across and are a mass of upturned bell-shaped flowers from June to August.

C.glomerata stands between 40cm and 70cm (16—28in) tall depending on the cultivar and has white or violet-blue flowers in clusters all the way up the stem in July and August. An established plant will spread about 40cm (16in) across and can be increased by division in spring. 'Superba' is a particularly striking violet-blue. All thrive in sun or semi-shade on any type of soil provided they have plenty of moisture.

C.lactiflora and C.latifolia favour a sunny position on rich, deeply dug, moist soil and welcome a mulch of well-rotted compost each autumn. In flower, C.lactiflora cultivars such as the flesh-pink 'Lodden Anna' or the lavender-blue C.lactiflora itself stand up to 150cm (5ft) tall with a spread of about 80cm (2¾ft). C.latifolia hybrids range from the dwarf lavender-blue 'Pouffe' at 25cm (10in) tall and 10cm (4in) across to the smoky-blue 'Gloaming' and the pure snowy-white 'White Ladies' which usually attain a height of about 100cm (3¼ft) and a spread of 60cm (2ft). Both groups make attractive and elegant material for flower arrangements with their graceful, feather-light spikes of bell-shaped blooms.

   6–8

SUMMER

Caryopteris × *clandonensis*

'Ferndown'

This attractive hybrid makes a handsome, mauve-flowering shrub which is usually maintained at a height and spread of about 100cm by 100cm (3¼ by 3¼ ft) since it must be pruned back to the base of the year-old growth every March. It thrives in full sun on any good garden soil, but does particularly well on chalk. The clone 'Arthur Simmonds', named after the man who made the original cross, is seldom offered nowadays, but 'Ferndown', 'Heavenly Blue' and 'Kew Blue' are usually easily obtainable and all have the characteristic, aromatic, grey-green foliage and masses of bloom.

 6–7

Catalpa bignonioides

C.bignonioides

The **Indian Bean Tree** is a very ornamental tree for an open site on well-drained soil and is usually one of the last in the garden to open its leaves. Within ten years it will make a dome-shaped, short-trunked tree of about 6m (20ft) tall and 4m (13ft) across, but will ultimately attain a height of about 20m (66ft) and a spread of 15m (50ft). The spikes of white and purple foxglove-like flowers are not produced on young trees but an established specimen will flower in July and August. The long seedpods that give the tree its nickname appear in autumn. It has huge, heart-shaped leaves, and as well as the plain, green-leafed species there is also a golden-leafed form, 'Aurea'.

 7–8

99

SUMMER

Ceanothus

'Gloire de Versailles'

Californian Lilacs are attractive shrubs for growing against a south-facing wall. Most species and hybrids are lime-tolerant but they really do best on free-draining, acid soils. The evergreen ones should only ever be lightly pruned immediately after flowering. They will grow up to 5m (16ft) tall by 2m (6½ft) across (tie them firmly to the wall). 'Delight' is one of the hardiest and covers itself in rich blue flowers in May. The deciduous ones, such as 'Gloire de Versailles' or 'Topaz', should be pruned back to within two or three buds of the old wood in early spring, and seldom grow more than 180cm (6ft) tall by 180cm across.

🌺 5 or 7 ○ ◗

Centaurea dealbata

'John Coutts'

'Steenbergii'

These attractive perennial relatives of the common cornflower grow well in hot, dry, sunny sites and are quite unfussy as to soil type. The plants in flower stand about 75cm (30in) tall with a spread of 40cm (16in) and bloom almost continuously from June to August. Clumps can easily be increased by division in spring or autumn. Two of the most popular cultivars are the bright pink 'John Coutts' and the deep, rosy-crimson 'Steenbergii', both of which have creamy-coloured centres to their flowers. Their long-lasting qualities in water also make them very popular as cut flowers.

🌺 6–8 ○ ◗

SUMMER

Centranthus ruber 'Coccineus'

'Coccineus'

Many reference works and catalogues spell this genus *Kentranthus*, but most gardeners just call it **Valerian** anyway and ignore the botanical disputes. It is a marvellous plant for a hot, dry spot in full sun and can sometimes be seen growing out of a crack in an old wall. The 80cm (2¾ ft) tall clumps of brilliant red flowers make a long-lasting feature, often blooming from June through into September. It is fond of lime and some should be added when planting if the soil is acid. An established plant will be about 50cm (20in) across, but it will also seed itself in the surrounding area.

 6–9 ○ ◗

Ceratostigma willmottianum

C.willmottianum

Except in very mild areas, this delightful little blue-flowered shrub is best grown against a south- or west-facing wall. They succeed in any dry, sunny, well-drained site on any type of soil. The bright china-blue flowers appear in July and often continue into the autumn. In March, the shrubby growth must be pruned back to within one or two buds of the old wood: this will maintain the shrub at a summer height of about 100cm (3¼ ft) and a width of about 80cm (2¾ ft) and ensure a good display of flowers. There is the added bonus of handsome, red-tinted foliage in autumn.

 7–9 ○ ◗

SUMMER

Choisya ternata

C.ternata

The **Mexican Orange Blossom** was introduced into Britain around 1825. It forms an impressive evergreen shrub up to 2m (6½ft) high and 2m across after ten or twelve years. Being tolerant of all soils and equally happy in sun or shade, it is a very popular choice as a specimen shrub. However, it can sometimes be damaged by cold winter winds. The aromatic, glossy green foliage makes a handsome background to the clusters of sweet-smelling white flowers that are borne from May until late June. Straggly shoots should be pruned in late spring.

🌸 5-6 ◑ 💧💧

Chrysanthemum maximum

'Wirral Supreme'

'Snowcap'

Shasta Daisies are invaluable perennials for the centre or back of the herbaceous border. Depending on the cultivar, they stand between 60cm and 90cm (2—3ft) tall and a well-established clump can be as much as 100cm (3¼ft) across — although it is best to lift and divide the clumps every third or fourth year in spring, replanting only the young growth from around the edge. They succeed readily in any fertile garden soil and do equally well in sun or partial shade. The large double flowered cultivars 'Esther Read' and 'Wirral Supreme' are very popular and make good cut flowers, and the lower-growing 'Snowcap' is also becoming widely popular. They flower from July to September.

🌸 7—9 ◑ 💧💧

SUMMER

Cistus × corbariensis

C. x corbariensis

This attractive little evergreen is one of the hardiest of the **Rock Roses**. It thrives in a hot, sunny position on poor, free-draining soil and does particularly well on chalk. It will eventually form a dome-shaped shrub about 100cm (3¼ ft) tall by 100cm across and for most of June and July will be studded with crimson-tipped buds which open to pure white flowers with a creamy-yellow flush at the base of the petals. Except for the removal of dead or weak shoots in March, it should not be pruned. It may die in a hard winter.

 5-6 ○ ◗

Clematis jackmannii Hybrids

'Hagley Hybrid'

This handsome group of large flowered, hybrid **Clematis** offers a wide choice of cultivars suitable for training up a trellis or through shrubs and trees. They flower in late summer on their new growth and should be pruned back to a couple of strong buds about 30cm (12in) from the ground every February. A cool, moist, shaded root-run is important to them but they like an open, sunny aspect for the flowering stems, so it is often best to cover the roots with a stone slab or plant a low-growing shrub or some hostas round their base. The most popular cultivars include 'Jackmannii', 'Hagley Hybrid' and 'Comtesse de Bouchaud'.

'Comtesse de Bouchard'

 7–9 ◑ ◗◗

103

SUMMER

Clematis lanuginosa and patens Hybrids

'Vyvian Pennell'

'Nelly Moser'

'Lasurstern'

This group of large flowered, hybrid **Clematis** bloom in late May. They flower on short growths made from the previous year's wood and the only pruning required is to remove the old flowering shoots as soon as the flowers have faded. Some double cultivars such as 'Vyvian Pennell' and 'Proteus' produce a second flush of single flowers in autumn. Other popular cultivars include 'W.E.Gladstone', 'Nelly Moser', 'Lasurstern' and 'The President'. Like jackmannii hybrids they like their roots in the shade and their heads in the sunshine, with plenty of water during dry spells.

 5–6 and 9

Convolvulus cneorum

C.cneorum

This delightful little, silver-leafed evergreen shrub is a most effective plant for a sunny, well-drained spot in the rock garden or at the edge of a path. In early June it is covered with white, funnel-shaped flowers flushed with pink on the reverse and it generally continues to open a few flowers right through the summer. It tolerates any soil type but may sometimes be killed off in a severe winter, so it is worth taking a few cuttings in June or July and rooting them in pots in a coldframe just in case. It rarely exceeds 60 cm (24in) high or 80cm (2¾ft) across, and dead or untidy shoots can be pruned out in March.

 6

SUMMER

Coreopsis grandiflora and *Coreopsis verticillata*

C.grandiflora 'Mayfield Giant'

C.verticillata 'Grandiflora'

These attractive perennials succeed easily in full sun, but dislike being overfed. The chief difference lies in their foliage: *C.grandiflora* has narrow, strap-like leaves while *verticillata* has finely divided, feathery ones. Cultivars of *C.grandiflora* vary from the 80cm (2¾ft) tall 'Mayfield Giant' with a spread of 60cm (24in) across, to the dwarf 'Goldfink' ('Goldfinch') at only 25cm (10in) tall and spreading about 20cm (8in). One of the named cultivars of *C.verticillata* is confusingly called 'Grandiflora' which generally grows about 60cm (24in) tall with a spread of 30cm (12in). There is also 'Zagreb' which is much more compact.

🌺 6–10 ○ ◆◆

Cornus kousa chinensis

C.kousa chinensis

This handsome, wide-spreading **Dogwood** is a most striking sight in June. The flowers themselves are insignificant but each is surrounded by four paper-white bracts which give the appearance of four huge extra petals. The shrub will grow readily in most soils, including frequently waterlogged ones, and flourishes equally well in sun or semi-shade. Within ten years it will stand about 2m (6½ft) tall with a spread of about 180cm (6ft) but its ultimate height will be about 3.5m (12ft) and spread 3m (10ft). The foliage turns a brilliant scarlet-bronze in autumn except on shallow, chalky soils.

🌺 6 ◑ ◆◆◆

Crambe cordifolia

C. cordifolia

This ornamental **Seakale** is a most statuesque herbaceous perennial and is best seen in an island bed in the centre of a lawn or some other open sunny situation where it can be viewed from all sides. An established plant will have a mound of huge, wavy-edged, grey-green leaves standing about 80cm (2¾ft) tall and spreading up to 180cm (6ft). The tall stems of graceful, fragrant white flowers often reach as high as 2m (6½ft) and bloom from May to July. It is very deep rooted and happy in any type of soil, but once established is almost impossible to eliminate. It is a good alternative to acanthus or pampas grass.

🌹 5–7 ○ ♦♦

Crocosmia × crocosmiiflora and Crocosmia masonorum

C. × crocosmiiflora

C. masonorum 'Lucifer'

Although these are all frequently referred to as **Montbretia**, it is really only the older C. × crocosmiiflora cultivars that were known by that name. They usually grow between 45cm and 60cm (18-24in) tall and the corms multiply themselves rapidly. A couple of dozen soon form a clump 60cm (24in) across. The C. masonorum cultivars, such as the brilliant orange 'Firebird', grow 80cm (2¾ft) tall and multiply themselves less rapidly. A new race of hybrids which are a true flame-red has also begun to emerge with the 100cm (3¼ft) tall 'Lucifer' as the most popular so far. All thrive in well-drained soil in sun or partial shade, blooming in late summer.

🌹 8–10 ◑ ♦♦

SUMMER

Cytisus battandieri and *Cytisus scoparius*

C.*battandieri*

C *scoparius* 'Dorothy Walpole'

The **Moroccan Broom,** *C.battandieri*, is an attractive alternative to the **Common Broom**. Its brilliant yellow, pineapple-scented flowers are highly ornamental, growing against a south-facing wall in July. It will grow about 3m (10ft) tall by 2m (6½ft) across and prefers quick-draining sandy soils but will tolerate a little lime. The common broom, *C.scoparius*, is smaller growing, usually about 150cm (5ft) tall by 150cm across and flowers in late May or June. It also demands light sandy soils in full sun and should be lightly pruned after flowering to discourage seed production.

 5–6 ○ ◆

Daboecia cantabrica

'Atropurpurea'

The **Irish Heath** is a most attractive spreading shrub for sunny, well-drained, lime-free sites. The large bell-shaped flowers bloom from June until well into the autumn. Long-established and reliable cultivars include the white 'Alba' and the rich purple 'Atropurpurea'. These will both grow to about 60cm (24in) tall and spread about 40cm (16in) within five years, but the crimson flowered 'William Buchanan' will attain only half that size. Being a little less invasive than other heathers, they associate more easily with herbaceous plants and dwarf deciduous shrubs. The spikes of dead flowers should be trimmed off.

 6–9 ○ ◆

SUMMER

Daphne × burkwoodii

D. x burkwoodii

This rapid-growing, semi-evergreen shrub is a great favourite for its pale pink, sweetly scented flowers which cluster along the branches in May and June. Within ten years it will attain its full height of 100cm (3¼ft) and 100cm spread. It thrives in an open position but will tolerate light shade and does equally well in acid or alkaline soils. A cool, moist root-run is important so plenty of compost or leafmould must be dug in before planting. A spring mulch of the same is also beneficial. No pruning is required except to remove dead wood or weak, straggly shoots in March.

🌹 5–6 ◑ ♦♦

Delphinium Pacific Hybrids

'Galahad'

'Black Knight'

These tall, aristocratic perennials look magnificent at the back of a border when in flower between July and August. The usual height of this particular strain is about 120cm to 150cm (4-5ft) and it has a spread of 50cm (20in). They grow best in a sunny position, in deeply dug, well-manured soil and should be supported to prevent wind damage. A well-placed slug trap in spring will prevent the emerging foliage from being nibbled to extinction. Cultivars such as 'Black Knight', the pure white 'Galahad' and the royal-purple 'King Arthur' are popular in England. If the main spike is cut out after flowering, secondary spikes will flower in September.

🌹 6–9 ◑ ♦♦

SUMMER

Desfontainea spinosa

D.spinosa

This beautiful, slow-growing, Chilean evergreen is not entirely hardy and should be grown in a semi-shaded position against a west-facing wall in all but the mildest areas. The foliage is very like holly, but in late summer it bears trumpet-shaped flowers, scarlet outside and yellow inside. It prefers lime-free soils with plenty of compost incorporated before planting. Within ten years it will be about 150cm (5ft) tall and 120cm (4ft) broad and its ultimate spread is not much more than this. Remove dead or straggly shoots in late March.

 8 ◑ ◆◆

Deutzia × hybrida

The cross between *D.discolor* and *D.longifolia* made in the Lemoine nursery at Nancy in the late 1920s has given rise to a number of attractive clones. All will grow to about 2m (6½ft) tall with a spread of about 150cm (5ft) within twelve or fifteen years. They thrive on any fertile garden soil in sun or partial shade and flower in June and July on one-year-old wood, so the flowering shoots must be pruned back to within 2cm or 3cm (1-1¼ in) of the main branch as soon as the blossom has faded. Popular cultivars include the mauve-pink 'Magicien' (usually offered as 'Magician') and the rose-pink 'Mont Rose'. 'Contraste' is also occasionally offered.

'Magicien'

 5–6 ◑ ◆◆

SUMMER

Dianthus Garden Pinks

'Doris'

'Prudence'

These free-flowering, sweet-smelling little perennials have been favourites in the garden since Elizabethan times. In common with most silver foliage plants they require an open sunny position and well-drained soil. They also appreciate a little lime dug into the soil if the garden is acid. There are double and single flowered cultivars, their heights can vary from 15cm to 30cm (6-12in) and they spread up to 40cm (16in) across. The white, double flowered 'Dad's Favourite' with its crimson eye is very popular, and the rose-pink 'Doris' is valued for its long succession of flowers from June to September.

 6–10 ○ ◗◗

Dictamnus fraxinella

D.fraxinella

This attractive perennial is sometimes referred to as *D.albus* 'Purpureus', but to save dispute gardeners simply call it **Burning Bush**. The 75cm (30in) tall spikes of rosy-purple flowers bloom from June to late August above a 40cm (16in) wide clump of pale green leaves which give the plant its nickname: they give off an aromatic vapour which can be set alight on still, sunny days and will burn off without harming the plant. They thrive in a sunny or lightly shaded spot on any fertile garden soil, but once planted should not be disturbed. A light spring dressing of general purpose fertilizer is beneficial. A white flowered form is occasionally offered.

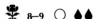 8–9 ○ ◗◗

SUMMER

Digitalis purpurea

D.purpurea

Strictly speaking, the **Foxglove** is a hardy biennial but some plants do flower for a second or third year and there are always new seedlings coming up to take over from the old plants as they die off. They are wonderful plants for sun or partial shade and tolerate all soil types. They usually stand up to 120cm (4ft) tall and the rosette of spear-shaped leaves at the base is usually about 40cm (16in) across on a plant of flowering age. Once they have finished flowering, leave the seedheads to ripen and give them a good shaking in November to scatter the new seed before cutting the stem for the bonfire.

Echinops ritro

E.ritro

The **Globe Thistle** is a magnificent plant for the centre of a sunny border. In flower it stands up to 100cm (3¼ ft) tall and an established plant is usually about 80cm (2¾ ft) across. The deeply indented dark green foliage with its silvery underside is very handsome, and the tall grey flower stems with their ball of steel-blue flowers make a striking contrast to other border perennials. They will thrive on any fertile garden soil, either acid or alkaline, and will tolerate some shade, although they look their best in full sun. A large clump can be divided into two or three new plants in early spring as the growth emerges.

SUMMER

Eremurus bungei and *Eremurus robustus*

E.robustus

E.bungei

Foxtail Lilies are imposing perennials for a sunny site sheltered from summer gales. *E.bungei* grows up to 150cm (5ft) high, and *E.robustus* up to 2.5m (8ft) tall. Their foliage can grow up to 100cm (3¼ ft) across. The flowers of *E.bungei* are golden-yellow but virtually scentless, and the pale pink flowers of *E.robustus* are very sweet-smelling. They are quite unfussy as to soil type and the crowns should be planted in October at least 15cm (6in) deep in heavily-manured soil. Division of large clumps can be undertaken in October.

   7 ○ ◖◗

Erica cinerea and *Erica vagans*

E.cinerea 'C. D. Eason'

E.vagans 'Lyonesse'

The **Scotch Heath**, *E.cinerea*, and the **Cornish Heath**, *E.vagans*, are excellent, weed-suppressing ground cover for well-drained positions on lime-free soil. There is almost as much colour choice in the foliage of the various cultivars as there is in their flowers, with bronze, golden, silver or sea-green-leafed plants offering white, pink, magenta or purple flowers. On average *E.cinerea* is between 20cm and 30cm (8-12in) tall with a spread of up to 60cm (24in). 'C.D.Eason', 'Purple Beauty' and 'Hookstone White' are popular *E.cinerea* cultivars, while 'Mrs D.F.Maxwell', 'Lyonesse' and 'St Kevenne' are popular *E.vagans* cultivars.

   8–10 ○ ◖

SUMMER

Erigeron

'Charity'

'Darkest of All'

'Foerster's Liebling'

The daisy-like flowers of this cheerful perennial are an attractive sight in the centre or at the front of the border. All of the cultivars flower between June and August and require a sunny position in free-draining soil. They range from 45cm to 60cm (18—24in) in height and spread between 30cm and 40cm (12-16in). The colours vary from the light pink 'Charity' and pale blue 'Prosperity' to the deep violet-blue 'Darkest of All' and the magenta 'Foerster's Liebling' (often offered as 'Foster's Darling'). They last well when cut for flower arrangements and, being non-invasive, can safely be planted without fear of their engulfing their neighbours.

🌺 6–8 ○ 💧💧

Eryngium giganteum

E.giganteum

Although a perennial, *E.giganteum* often adopts a biennial habit, renewing itself from self-sown seedlings every two or three years. It is often referred to as **Sea Holly** and sometimes as **Miss Wilmott's Ghost**. The whole plant is a striking silver-grey with flowers of a most attractive shade of steel-blue, and it invariably excites comment. It will flourish on any dry, well-drained soil provided it has a sunny position. Normally it will grow about 90cm (3ft) tall with a spread of 80cm (2¾ft) and it is a popular flower for cutting since it lasts well in water and contrasts handsomely with other garden flowers.

🌺 7–9 ○ 💧

Escallonia 'Iveyi' and 'C. F. Ball'

'C. F. Ball'

These colourful, June-flowering, semi-evergreen shrubs grow easily on any well-drained soil. They will grow to between 1.5m and 2.5m (5-8ft) tall and spread up to 1.5m (5ft) across. They are not always reliably hardy, and in cold districts should be grown within the protection of a wall or other shrubs. 'Iveyi' is white flowered and blooms for a long-lasting display, while 'C.F.Ball' is rich crimson with dark, glossy foliage that has a pleasantly aromatic smell when crushed. Prune out all shoots that have borne flowers as soon as the blossom has faded.

 6–8 ○ ♦♦

Eucryphia × *nymansensis*

'Nymansay'

This attractive but variable hybrid makes an interesting evergreen flowering tree up to 10m (33ft) tall with a spread of 6m (20ft) within twenty years. The large single white flowers with a central boss of golden stamens cluster along the branches in August and September. It will tolerate some lime in the soil, but not a lot, and it requires plenty of moisture. It favours a sheltered, sunny site and the root-run should be shaded. The clone most commonly offered is 'Nymansay' which is the original plant. 'Mount Usher' is also sometimes available and frequently produces double flowers but grows about 10 per cent larger than 'Nymansay'.

 8–9 ○ ♦♦

SUMMER

Fuchsia magellanica

'Riccartonii'

The most commonly-grown hardy **Fuchsia** is *F.magellanica* with its attractive scarlet-and-purple flowered cultivar 'Riccartonii' and coloured-foliage cultivars such as 'Variegata' and 'Versicolour'. They tolerate all soils so long as they have plenty of moisture, and they are equally happy in sun or shade. The flowers are usually an attractive combination of scarlet and deep violet and are produced freely throughout the summer. Size varies according to cultivar, with 'Riccartonii' being one of the largest at 180cm (6ft) tall by 150cm (5ft) across, down to the compact dwarf 'Pumila' at only 25cm (10in) tall and 40cm (16in) across.

There is also another group of hybrids, many of which have a good deal of *F.magellanica* in their parentage. Most grow to a dome-shaped shrub up to 80cm (2¾ft) tall and 80cm across. The warm yellow spring foliage of 'Golden Treasure' is very striking in the garden in April and May, gradually darkening to a light green as summer progresses. The scarlet and white 'Madame Cornelissen' has been a popular garden shrub for over 100 years, and the cream and magenta 'Eva Boerg' has proved equally popular since its introduction in the 1940s. The compact hybrid 'Tom Thumb' is much smaller, as its name implies, rarely exceeding 50cm (20in) in height or 50cm across. Care should be taken to see that the plants are kept well watered during their first year in the garden, and a spring mulch of peat or compost is beneficial.

'Madame Cornelissen'

 7–9

115

SUMMER

Gaillardia aristata Hybrids

'Mandarin'

'Goblin'

These gorgeous orange or yellow flowered perennials are very popular because they usually begin to bloom in June and continue right through to September if you keep snipping off the dead flowerheads. Most cultivars, such as the flame and orange 'Mandarin' or the bright tangerine 'Tommy', grow up to 90cm (3ft) tall with a spread of about 40cm (16in) but the dwarf cultivar 'Goblin' with its red-centred, golden-yellow flowers is only about 30cm (12in) tall and spreads only 15cm (6in). All cultivars like a sunny, well-drained site and tolerate any type of soil. Divide large clumps in spring.

🌺 6–9 ○ ◑

Galtonia candicans

G.candicans

The **Summer Hyacinth** (sometimes offered as *Hyacinthus candicans*) is a most attractive summer-flowering bulb for a sunny border. It is quite unfussy as to soil type provided that it is well drained. The spikes of white, sweetly scented, bell-shaped flowers appear in July and August, standing about 120cm (4ft) tall, and an established clump can be up to 60cm (24in) across. The bulbs should be planted in early spring 15cm (6in) deep and about 20cm (8in) apart. After a few years, the bulbs can be lifted and separated in autumn once the foliage has died down. In areas prone to severe frosts, a winter mulch of bracken or leafmould is a wise precaution.

🌺 7–8 ◑ ◑◑

SUMMER

Gaultheria procumbens

The **Creeping Wintergreen** is a
marvellous evergreen carpeting
shrub for moist, shady areas. It
is not lime-tolerant and prefers
peaty soils to any other kind,
but will succeed on neutral
soils if mulched annually with
peat. It never grows more than
10cm (4in) tall but will rapidly
form a mat of weedproof
foliage up to 100cm (3¼ ft)
across. The tiny pink and white
flowers that smother the bush
in July and August are
followed in autumn by bright
crimson berries which look
very handsome against the
dark green, leathery foliage.
Apart from pruning out any
dead wood in February or
March, it requires no attention.

G.procumbens

 7–8

Genista hispanica and Genista lydia

G.hispanica

Both of these low-growing
shrubs make attractive mounds
of brilliant yellow flowers in
early summer. Each will grow
up to 100cm (3¼ ft) tall and
spread up to 150cm (5ft)
across. They thrive best in acid
or neutral soils but they are
lime-tolerant. G.hispanica,
Spanish Gorse, is the more
compact of the two, forming a
dense, spiny cushion while
G.lydia makes a hummock of
arching, grey-green stems. They
demand sunny, well-drained
sites and require no pruning
except the removal of dead
wood and weak or unwanted
shoots which is best done in
early March.

G.lydia

 7 ○

SUMMER

Geranium

G.pratense
'Johnson's Blue'

G.sanguineum

Crane's Bills are extremely useful summer-flowering perennials for the herbaceous border and must never be confused with their relatives *pelargoniums* (so often miscalled *geraniums*) whose needs and habits are quite different. There are a number of species and cultivars available and they range in height from the majestic 60cm (24in) tall *G.pratense* with a spread of about 30cm (12in), and the wide-spreading 'Johnson's Blue' only 40cm (16in) high but as much as 80cm (2¾ft) across, down to the semi-prostrate *G.sanguineum* whose magenta flowers stand only 25cm (10in) high and which spreads up to about 30cm (12in). All are valued for their easy-going nature.

 6–8 ◑ ◆◆

Geum × borisii and Geum chiloense

G.chiloense
'Lady Strathden'

G. × borisii

These adaptable, free-flowering perennials come in various shades of scarlet, orange and yellow and succeed on any good garden soil. If they are happy with their position they will increase by seeding themselves around. G. × *borisii* makes a neat mound some 30cm (12in) high by 30cm across and bears brilliant orange flowers in June, often giving a second flush of bloom in late August. The most commonly offered cultivars of *G.chiloense* are 'Mrs Bradshaw' and 'Lady Strathden'. Both stand about 60cm (24in) tall with a spread of 30cm (12in).

 6 and 8 ◑ ◆◆

Gladiolus byzantinus, Gladiolus nanus and Large Dutch Hybrid Gladioli

G.nanus

'Peter Pears'

Large Dutch Hybrid **Gladioli** look magnificent at the back of the border, and the two smaller species mix well with other border plants. Where winter frosts are severe, lift them each autumn and store in a cool dry place, replanting the following April. They need full sun and free-draining soil. *G.byzantinus* grows about 60cm (24in) tall while *G.nanus* varies between 45cm and 60cm (18–24in) tall. Small corms should be planted 8cm (3in) deep and 12cm (5½in) apart, and the larger ones 12cm (5½in) deep and 20cm (8in) apart.

🌺 7 ○ ◆

Gypsophila paniculata

'Bristol Fairy'

Baby's Breath is a graceful, free-flowering perennial which displays an airy mist of tiny flowers from June to September. Cultivars such as the white 'Bristol Fairy' and the shell-pink 'Flamingo' stand about 120cm (4ft) tall in flower and the wide, branching stems cover an area up to 100cm (3¼ft) across, but there are more compact cultivars such as 'Compacta Plena' and 'Rosy Veil' which make a neat mound about 25cm (10in) high and 25cm across. They are lime-loving plants and some should be added when planting if your soil is acid. They resent disturbance so propagation is best done by taking cuttings in July.

🌺 6 ◐ ◆◆

Hebe

H.speciosa
'Veitchii'

H.pinguifolia 'Pagei'

There are many species and cultivars of this attractive evergreen genus. They are not always frost hardy but before uprooting an apparently dead bush after a bad winter, check that there is no fresh growth emerging at the base. Simply prune the damaged shoots back to ground level. *H.speciosa* cultivars such as 'Gauntlettii' and 'Veitchii' ('Alicia Amherst') make good rounded shrubs 150cm (5ft) tall by 150cm across, while *H.pinguifolia* 'Pagei' makes an attractive spreading mound up to 30cm (12in) tall and 80cm (2¾ft) across. All species and cultivars will grow readily on any well-drained fertile garden soil.

 5–7 ◑ ♦♦

Helenium autumnale

'Coppelia'

Sneezeweed is an invaluable plant for providing colour in the border at a time when many other perennials are coming to the end of their display. They require an open, sunny site and grow readily on any free-draining soil. Some can be a bit on the sprawling side but most of the modern cultivars have a neat habit and make good solid blocks of colour in August and September. The pure yellow 'Butterpat' stands 100cm (3¼ft) tall and the warm orange 'Coppelia' is 90cm (3ft) tall and both will spread about 40cm (16in) across. 'Golden Youth' is shorter growing and flowers earlier. Plants can be increased by division in spring.

'Golden Youth' 8–9 ○ ♦

SUMMER

Helianthemum nummularium

'The Bride'

'Raspberry
Ripple'

Rock Roses make very
attractive, rapid-growing dwarf
shrubs for the rock garden or
as ground cover on an open
site. They thrive in hot, dry,
sunny positions on poor soil.
Their height can vary between
10cm and 30cm (4-12in)
according to cultivar, and a
well-established plant can
spread up to 100cm (3¼ ft)
across over a period of ten
years. Flower colours range
mostly from butter yellow to
deep orange but there are pink
and crimson cultivars as well.
'Ben Nevis' is a golden-orange,
'Wisley Primrose' a clear yellow
with grey foliage and
'The Bride' is creamy-white
with a yellow centre.

 6–8 ○ ◗

Helichrysum × *hybridum* and *Helichrysum bellidioides*

H. x hybridum 'Sulphur Light'

H.bellidioides

These two perennials are
attractive and unusual
additions to any garden. *H. ×
hybridum* 'Sulphur Light'
(*H.augustifolium*) has downy,
silver, aromatic leaves and
small clusters of sulphur-yellow
flowers from June to
September. *H.bellidioides* is a
charming white flowered rock
garden plant, rarely more than
5cm (2in) tall and forming a
spreading mat of silvery foliage
covered in crisp white flowers
in July and August. Both plants
need a sunny position on poor
but well-drained soil. They
loathe winter wet, so protect
them from November to
March.

 6–9 ○ ◗

Hemerocallis Hybrids

'Pink Damask'

'Stafford'

Day Lilies are so called because their individual flowers seldom last more than one day, but new ones are continually opening giving colour fron June to September. Most cultivars stand between 60cm and 80cm (24-33in) tall and a well-established clump can be as muçh as 100cm (3¼ ft) across. They grow easily in any good garden soil in sun or semi-shade. Intensive cross-breeding of these perennials has produced an astonishing number of colours. They resent disturbance, so once you have planted them leave well alone except for a spring mulch of garden compost.

 7–9

Heuchera sanguinea

H.sanguinea

This is an excellent ground-covering, evergreen perennial for sun or semi-shade and grows easily on any well-drained garden soil. The dark green foliage forms a mat about 10cm (4in) high from which the flower stems emerge in June and July, usually standing between 60cm and 75cm (24-30in) tall. The flowers are usually shades of pink, but there are also white-and-green-coloured flowers, notably 'Green Ivory'. 'Palace Purple' takes its name from its rich purple foliage, has white flowers and is a hybrid from H.americanum. A spring mulch of peat or well-rotted compost will ensure a vigorous flowering display in summer.

6–8

SUMMER

Hibiscus syriacus

'Blue Bird'

'Woodbridge'

The **Tree Hollyhock** is a hardy deciduous shrub which will ultimately grow to about 3m (10ft) tall and 3m across. In August and September it is covered with gorgeous trumpet-shaped flowers. It opens its leaves later than most shrubs, so underplant with spring bulbs. It grows happily on any well-drained soil in a sunny position. No pruning is required apart from a brief session in February to remove any crossing or weak shoots or dead wood. The deep, blue-mauve 'Blue Bird' is widely regarded as the best of the blue-flowered cultivars, and other colours include the very pale pink 'Hamabo' and the deep rose 'Woodbridge'.

 8 ○ ◆

Hoheria sexstylosa

This exotic **New Zealand Ribbonwood** makes a tall evergreen shrub or, with some attention in its early stages of growth, a delightful small tree. Its maximum height is about 6m (20ft) and its spread 3m (10ft). The dark green, saw-edged leaves have a downy silver underside and form a perfect background for the large clusters of pure white flowers that open in July and August. It requires a sunny well-drained position but will tolerate any soil type and, apart from cutting out dead or awkwardly-placed shoots in March, it needs no pruning.

 7–8 ○ ◆

H.sexstylosa

SUMMER

Hosta

'Frances Williams'
'Royal Standard'

The **Plantain Lilies** are valued as ground cover for moist, shaded or semi-shaded sites. The huge leaves of some of the cultivars are very striking and there are also a number with interestingly coloured or variegated foliage. Plain green- or blue-leafed ones can even be grown in full sun, provided they get plenty of moisture. Hosta flowers are usually either white or lilac-mauve and heights vary according to cultivar from the 30cm (12in) tall 'Thomas Hogg' with white-edged, dark green leaves to the 90cm (3ft) tall variegated *H.sieboldiana* 'Frances Williams'. 'Royal Standard' has 90cm (3ft) tall spikes of sweetly scented flowers in August, but most are grown for their foliage

🌺 7–8 ● ▲▲▲

Hydrangea macrophylla

'Hamburgh'

'Blue Wave'

Common Hydrangeas fall into two groups: Hortensia or Mop Head cultivars which produce globular heads of white, pink or blue flowers, and Lacecaps which have flat heads of tiny fertile flowers surrounded by a ring of large sterile florets. Mop Head cultivars such as 'Hamburgh' vary in colour according to the soil: blue colouring will disappear on chalky soils, changing to a dusty pink unless treated by watering in a solution of salts of iron and aluminium. Of the Lacecaps, 'Blue Wave' and 'White Wave' are very popular. All grow best in an open position in moist, well-manured soils. Dead flowerheads should be pruned back to the old wood in March.

🌺 7–10 ◑ ▲▲

SUMMER

Hydrangea petiolaris

H.petiolaris

This vigorous, self-clinging, climbing **Hydrangea** is an excellent shrub for clothing a north- or west-facing wall or to send scrambling up a large old tree. The flowers appear in June, and the bare mahogany-red stems look very handsome in winter. An established plant can reach as high as 25m (82ft) with a spread of 20m (66ft) if allowed to do so, but it can be kept in bounds by pruning in August. It will require four or five years to establish itself but is tolerant of any soil type provided that it gets plenty of moisture. A spring mulch of leafmould or compost around the base is beneficial.

 6 ● ◆◆

Hypericum calycinum

H.calycinum

The **Rose of Sharon** is a remarkably hardy, evergreen, ground-cover shrub for sun or shade. It is drought-tolerant and grows readily in any garden soil but does have a rather invasive nature and should not be grown in association with less robust plants which might get choked off after a couple of seasons. The bright golden-yellow flowers open in June and July. In order to keep it compact the plants should be pruned back hard with shears in early spring. It will usually grow to a height of about 40cm (16in) and its spread will be whatever you allow it to become since it roots the ends of its stems and forms new plants as it goes along.

 6–7 ● ◆◆

SUMMER

Incarvillea delavayi

I.delavayi

The **Trumpet Flower** is a most attractive, low-growing perennial for a sunny position at the front of the border. It requires a fairly moist soil, so plenty of compost or peat should be dug in before planting and a spring mulch of the same is a good idea. In flower the plant is about 45cm (18in) tall with a spread of 30cm (12in). In June and July the flower stems bearing rosy-pink blooms emerge from the centre of a clump of dark green foliage. Your stock can be increased either by division in early spring or by collecting the seed and sowing it the following April in a coldframe.

 6-7 ○ ◆◆

Iris, Dwarf, Intermediate and Tall Bearded

'Dancer's Veil'

'Small Wonder'

These attractive perennials succeed easily in a sunny, well-drained site on any fertile garden soil. Dwarf cultivars such as 'Blue Denim' or 'Lemon Flare' stand up to 30cm (12in) tall with a spread of about 20cm (8in) when established, while Intermediates like 'Small Wonder' stand up to 70cm (28in) tall with a spread of 40cm (16in). Tall cultivars such as 'Jane Phillips' and 'Dancer's Veil' stand between 90cm and 120cm (3-4ft) tall with a spread of up to 60cm (24in). The rhizomes should be planted partly exposed on the surface of the soil and congested clumps are best divided in July as soon as the flowers have finished. The Dwarfs flower in late spring, the Intermediates in mid-May and the Tall cultivars in June.

 6 ○ ◆

Iris kaempferi and *Iris pseudacorus*

I.pseudacorus

I.kaempferi

These two species are excellent plants for an open, boggy situation at the margin of a pool or stream but should not be permanently planted right in the water. The Japanese have raised many beautiful hybrids of *I.kaempferi* ranging in colour from white to royal purple, but the species is not lime-tolerant. *I.pseudacorus* is the **Common Flag** seen wild at the edge of many streams and ponds in Northern Europe and may be the original of the French *fleur-de-lys*.

I.kaempferi will usually attain 90cm (3ft) in height and form graceful clumps about 40cm (16in) across, while *I.pseudacorus* is usually about the same.

Itea ilicifolia

I.ilicifolia

This interesting Chinese evergreen with holly-like leaves is slightly tender and would be best growing against a sheltered, west-facing wall in cold or exposed areas. The small, greenish-white flowers dangle in long sweet-smelling catkins in August and September, providing interest in late summer when most flowering shrubs are over. It is tolerant of any soil type provided that there is plenty of moisture available during the summer. A mature specimen of twenty years' growth will stand up to 3m (10ft) tall with a spread of 2m (6½ft) and it requires no pruning except the removal of dead shoots in March.

SUMMER

Kalmia latifolia

K. latifolia

The **Calico Bush** is a very pretty evergreen shrub which requires roughly the same conditions as rhododendrons and camellias, and indeed looks very attractive when grown alongside them. Within ten years it will form a low, dome-shaped bush about 180cm (6ft) tall by 150cm (5ft) across and in June the glossy, dark green foliage is almost submerged under clusters of bright sugar-pink flowers. The delightful dark pink clones 'Clementine Churchill' and 'Brilliant' can sometimes be obtained. They thrive in moist, acid, peaty soils in semi-shade. Take out any dead or straggly shoots in March or April.

Kniphofia uvaria

K. uvaria

Red Hot Pokers are in fact available in all shades from the pale, creamy-yellow of 'Maid of Orleans' through the yellow and orange 'Royal Standard' to the deep orange-reds such as 'Fiery Fred' and 'Samuel's Sensation'. Plant in autumn in well-manured soil in a sunny position, then cover for the winter with a mulch of bracken litter or leafmould to protect from frost. Their normal height is 90cm to 110cm (3—3½ft) and the clumps of grey-green grass-like foliage stand up to 80cm (2¾ft) across. The semi-hardy K.galpinnii is sometimes offered and requires similar conditions but grows only 75cm (30in) tall and 40cm (16in) across. It is not suitable for cold, frosty districts.

SUMMER

Laburnum anagyroides and Laburnum × watereri 'Vossii'

L. x watereri 'Vossii'

The **Common Laburnum** L.anagyroides and its descendant 'Vossii' are very popular June-flowering trees. Their brilliant golden flowers borne in long dangling chains are very striking and even quite young plants bloom within a year or two of planting. 'Vossii' is often preferred because it produces very little seed and since all laburnum seed is poisonous, the less there is around the better (the foliage is also poisonous). They grow happily in any type of soil in an open situation. The ultimate height is about 8m (26ft) with a spread of 5m (16ft).

Lavandula spica and Lavandula stoechas

L.spica 'Hidcote'

L.stoechas

L.spica cultivars (also offered as L.augustifolia) are the **Old English Lavenders**, except for the vigorous cultivar 'Vera' which is usually called **Dutch Lavender**. All have grey, aromatic foliage and flower colours vary. The smallest, such as 'Munstead' and 'Hidcote', seldom grow taller than 60cm (24in) or spread more than 80cm (2¾ ft), but 'Grappenhall' and 'Vera' can be up to 100cm (3¼ ft) tall and spread 120cm (4ft) across. **French Lavender**, L.stoechas, has light green foliage and deep purple flowers but is only half-hardy. It makes a small bushy clump 35cm (14in) tall and 30cm (12in) across.

SUMMER

Lavatera olbia 'Rosea'

'Rosea'

The **Shrubby Mallow** is botanically somewhere between a shrub and a herbaceous perennial so it is confusingly found in the shrub department of some nurseries and the herbaceous department of others. Its top growth dies each winter and it should be cut back to the base each spring. The 160cm (5¼ ft) tall sprays of bright pink, hollyhock-like flowers bloom almost continuously from June to October. It succeeds best on poor, free-draining soil in a sunny position. It is not a particularly long-lived plant, so it is best to take a few cuttings each August to ensure continuity although it will also seed itself around as well.

 6–9 ○ ◗◗

Leptospermum scoparium

'Nichollsii'

The **New Zealand Tea Tree** is a delightful twiggy, evergreen shrub which covers itself in blossom in June. It is happiest in full sun on acid or neutral soils and in cold areas needs the protection of a south-facing wall or other shrubs. In mild coastal districts it can grow up to 4m (13ft) tall by 2m (6½ ft) across but in most areas it is somewhat smaller. There are a number of named cultivars offered with flower colours ranging from white and pale pink to deep red. 'Red Damask' is a popular favourite for its deep cherry-red double flowers and is one of the hardiest. 'Nichollsii' is also a good plant with bright crimson flowers and purple-bronze foliage.

 6 ○ ◗◗

Leycesteria formosa

L.formosa

The **Himalayan Honeysuckle** is an interesting and unusual deciduous shrub for a shaded or semi-shaded position. It succeeds well in any fertile garden soil and the curious, hollow, bright green stems form a dense shrub about 180cm (6ft) tall by 150cm (5ft) across. The small white flowers are borne in drooping clusters from June to September but are almost hidden inside spectacular, wine-purple bracts. Blackish berries are produced freely after flowering and many drop and germinate the following year; more will be carried off by birds. Each spring the oldest branches should be pruned out at the base to allow newer growth to ripen.

6–9 ● ◆◆

Liatris spicata

'Kobold'

Gayfeather is a valuable, late-flowering perennial which blooms in August and September, helping to prolong the summer display. In flower it stands about 60cm (24in) tall and an established plant will have a spread of about 30cm (12in). They prefer poor, free-draining soil in full sun and the plants can be increased by dividing in spring just as they begin to emerge. The cultivar most commonly offered is 'Kobold' which has particularly dense spikes of rich mauve flowers, but one can occasionally find a white form, 'Alba', in some specialist nurseries.

8–9 ○ ◆

SUMMER

Ligularia

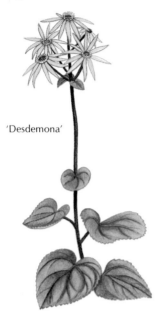

'Desdemona'

There are several species and hybrids of these striking perennial plants and all make highly ornamental plants for a moist spot at the edge of a pool or stream in sun or light shade. They thrive on any soil type and need little attention once they are planted, although one or two can be rather invasive. 'Desdemona' is an attractive, orange-yellow flowered cultivar and stands about 120cm (4ft) tall with a spread of 40cm (16in), but two or three plants will swiftly fill up a space of more than 100cm (3¼ ft) square. 'Sungold' is less rampant and only 90cm (3ft) tall by about 30cm (12in) with bright golden-yellow flowers. The main flowering period is July and August.

Lilium auratum and Lilium regale

L.auratum

L.regale

Lilies are the most popular summer-flowering bulbs. These two sweetly scented species grow fairly tall, *L.auratum* usually attaining 2m to 2.5m (6½−8ft) in height while *L.regale* is normally up to 150cm (5ft) high but may grow taller. The plant is never more than 30cm (12in) across but it is most effective planted in groups. The bulbs should be planted in moist, rich, lime-free, well-drained soil as soon as they are obtained, setting them at least 15cm (6in) deep and 20cm (8in) apart. They prefer an open situation with their roots in the shade but flowerheads in the sun for as least part of the day.

SUMMER

Lilium hansonii and *Lilium martagon*

L.hansonii

L.martagon

These two attractive, lime-tolerant **Lilies** are excellent plants for semi-shaded sites among deciduous trees or tall shrubs. Both the rosy-purple (or white) *L.martagon* and the golden-orange *L.hansonii* will stand between 90cm and 150cm (3—5ft) tall. Each plant is about 20cm (8in) across but a well-established clump can be 100cm (3¼ft) square or more. The bulbs should be planted about 5cm (2in) deep and 25cm (10in) apart in groups of five or ten. They like moist, free-draining soil and an autumn mulch of well-rotted compost or leafmould.

 6—7 ◑ ♦♦

Lonicera × *americana* and *Lonicera periclymenum*

L.periclymenum

L. x americanum

L.periclymenum is the sweet-smelling **Woodbine** of English hedgerows. The two cultivars most commonly offered are 'Belgica' ('Early Dutch'), flowering in May and June and again at the end of summer, and 'Serotina' ('Late Dutch'), flowering from July to October. If permitted they can reach a height of 5m (16ft) and a spread of 6m (20ft) but can be kept in bounds by autumn pruning. *L.* × *americana* is a vigorous, sweet-smelling hybrid capable of attaining up to 9m (30ft) in height and spreading up to 6m (20ft). All are tolerant of any soil type provided they get plenty of moisture.

 5—7 ◑ ♦♦♦

Lupinus Russell Hybrids

Because of problems of disease, it is now best to obtain **Lupins** that have been raised from seed. This means that many of the popular old named cultivars are no longer commercially available but the Russell Strain provides a wide range of good clear colours. In flower they stand about 100cm (3¼ ft) tall with a spread of 40cm (16in) and are best planted in groups of three or five. They grow happily in sun or light shade on any fertile garden soil, flowering in late May or early June. The removal of the first flower spike as soon as the flowers have faded often encourages a second flush of bloom.

Russell Hybrids

Lychnis coronaria 'Atrosanguinea'

'Atrosanguinea'

This attractive grey-leafed perennial is easy to grow. The soft, felt-like foliage forms a ground-hugging rosette about 25cm (10in) across and from June to September sends up 30cm (12in) tall stems bearing rich magenta flowers. It grows readily on any well-drained garden soil and prefers a position in full sun. Once established it will seed itself around freely, making a substantial clump unless you weed out the seedlings in early summer. Very occasionally you may find the white form, *L.coronaria* 'Alba' offered.

Lysimachia punctata

This bright golden flowered herbaceous perennial, commonly known as as **Yellow Loosestrife,** is becoming a familiar sight along English river and canal banks where it has escaped from gardens and naturalized itself. It thrives in a moist site in sun or semi-shade and is quite unfussy as to soil type. An established clump will stand up to 80cm (33in) tall and 60cm (24in) across and flowers from June to late August. It can easily be propagated by division in spring but will, in any case, seed itself around, and you may find it spreading further than you want it to unless you weed out the seedlings before they establish themselves.

   6—8

L.punctata

Lythrum salicaria

The **Purple Loosestrife** is another invaluable herbaceous perennial for a moist, heavy, partially shaded soil, especially at the edge of a stream or pond. The brightly coloured flower spikes vary from the warm pink 'Robert' to the deep rosy-purple 'Firecandle' and 'The Beacon' and bloom from July to September. In flower the plant is usually between 60cm and 90cm (24—36in) tall and an established clump can be up to 90cm (36in) across. They can be increased by division in spring or by cuttings taken before flowering and grown on in a coldframe to be planted out in April or May the following year.

'Firecandle'

   7—9

SUMMER

Magnolia grandiflora

M.grandiflora

This magnificent evergreen **Magnolia** is often grown against a wall to make it flower more freely, but performs equally well as a free-standing specimen tree in mild or sheltered locations. It is lime-tolerant except on particularly thin, chalky soils and is relatively slow growing, attaining only 6m (20ft) in height with a spread of 4m (13ft) after twenty years. In maturity it will be more than four times that size, but that's a problem for your great-grandchildren, not you. The creamy-white, sweetly scented flowers open in ones and twos throughout the summer but do not appear on young specimens except on the clones 'Exmouth' and 'Goliath' which are therefore the most popular choice.

 3–10

Monarda didyma

'Croftway Pink'

'Cambridge Scarlet'

Bergamot is a popular herbaceous perennial which grows readily in rich moist soil in sun or partial shade. During June, July and August when the plant is in flower it stands about 90cm (36in) tall with a spread of 40cm (16in). Flower colour is mostly shades of pink and red from the rosy-purple 'Prairie Glow' and its even darker sister 'Prairie Night' to the soft pink 'Croftway Pink', but by far the most popular cultivar is the brilliantly coloured 'Cambridge Scarlet'. There is also a white cultivar 'Snow Maiden'. They must be kept liberally watered in periods of drought, and a spring mulch of compost is beneficial. The rootstock divides easily.

 6–8

SUMMER

Nepeta mussinii

N.mussinii

Catmint is a marvellous low-growing herbaceous perennial with silver-grey foliage and lavender-blue flowers. It does best in a sunny situation in light, free-draining soil at the front of the border and flowers freely from May to September if dead-headed regularly. Once flowering is finished the plant should be clipped over lightly with a pair of shears to keep it compact and tidy. Its normal height is around 30cm (12in) with a spread of 40cm (16in) but the clone 'Six Hills Giant' is twice that size and much more vigorous. Unfortunately, though, that particular clone is sterile and can only be propagated by cuttings taken in spring.

 🌺 5–9 ○ ◆

Oenothera missouriensis and Oenothera tetragona

O.missouriensis

These **Evening Primroses** are a good choice for light, well-drained soil in a sunny or semi-shaded position. *O.missouriensis* forms a spreading network of trailing stems about 60cm (24in) across and the flowers and foliage stand about 20cm (8in) high; *O.tetragona* forms a leafy clump about 45cm (18in) tall and 30cm (12in) across. Among the popular *O.tetragona* cultivars are 'Fireworks' with bright red buds that open to the characteristic sunshine-yellow flowers, and the large flowered 'Highlight'. Both species provide bold blocks of strong yellow colour from June to late August, and *O.missouriensis* has the added attraction of large, ornamental seedpods in autumn.

O.tetragona 'Fireworks'

 🌺 6–8 ◑ ◆

Olearia × haastii and Olearia macrodonta

O.macrodonta

These attractive New Zealand evergreen shrubs, often known as **Daisy Bushes**, are especially fond of chalky soils but will succeed easily on any other well-drained soil type provided that they have a sunny position. *O. × haastii* will eventually attain a height of 2.5m (8ft) with a spread of 1.5m (5ft) but spring frost damage in cold districts could well keep it much smaller than that. *O.macrodonta*, the **New Zealand Holly**, will attain up to 4m (13ft) in height in mild areas and could be trained as a small tree if desired; its maximum spread is about 2m (6½ ft). Both bear masses of fragrant white flowers, *O.macrodonta* in June followed by *O. × haastii* which blooms throughout July and August.

 6–8 ○

Paeonia lactiflora, Paeonia officinalis and Paeonia suffruticosa

P.officinalis
'Rubra Plena'

P.lactiflora
'Bowl of Beauty'

Herbaceous Paeonies
P.lactiflora and *P.officinalis* are tolerant of any soil type provided that the site has been deeply dug and plenty of compost or leafmould incorporated. They need an open position but are best shaded from the early morning sun. Set the crowns just a centimetre or two below the surface of the soil and, once planted, never disturb them. *P.officinalis* cultivars such as the white 'Alba Plena', the pink and white 'Lize van Veen' and the deep crimson 'Rubra Plena' normally bloom in late May,

while *P. lactiflora* cultivars such as the white 'Duchesse de Nemours', the gorgeous cream and pink 'Bowl of Beauty' and the rich pink 'Sarah Bernhardt' flower in June and July. Both species attain a height of up to 80cm (2¾ ft) and a well-established clump will have a spread of anything up to 100cm (3¼ ft). The **Moutan Paeony,** *P. suffruticosa* is a deciduous shrub and sometimes proves to be rather tender. In an open, sheltered position, shaded from early-morning sunshine, it can grow up to 2m (6½ ft) tall with a spread of about 2m after fifteen years. It grows particularly well on chalky soils. The huge silky flowers appear in May and June.

P. suffruticosa

 6–7

Papaver orientale

Oriental Poppies make a brilliant splash of colour in the herbaceous border from late May to August. They are happy in any fertile, well-drained soil and prefer a position in full sun. The flowerheads are often so large that their stems cannot support them properly and it is a good idea to provide the plant with staked support. Cultivars raised at the Perry nursery at Enfield, Middlesex, in the first half of this century still lead the field with 'Perry's White', the gorgeous salmon-pink 'Mrs Perry' and the brilliant orange 'Marcus Perry' as popular as ever. The plants normally stand between 75cm and 90cm (30—36in) tall in flower, and a well-established specimen is usually about 40cm (16in) across.

'Mrs Perry'

 6–8

SUMMER

Passiflora caerulea

P.caerulea

The blue **Passion Flower** is a vigorous semi-evergreen climber for a warm sunny wall. It is not always reliably hardy and should not be planted in areas prone to severe frost. Given a frame to climb upon it can rapidly attain a height of 5m or 6m (16—20ft) and a spread of about 4m (13ft) producing its exotic blue and white, slightly fragrant blooms from June until early autumn. It is tolerant of any soil type and normally requires a light pruning in March to remove any dead wood and weak or unwanted shoots. After a long, hot summer it may well produce a crop of bright orange, egg-shaped fruits which are perfectly safe to eat and make quite a pleasant jam.

 6–8 ○

Penstemon hartwegii (Syn. Penstemon gloxinioides) and Penstemon barbatus

P.hartwegii 'Firebird'

These brightly coloured herbaceous perennials need a sunny, sheltered, well-drained position at the front of the border. Most cultivars of P.hartwegii grow to about 60cm (24in) tall although 'King George' attains 80cm (33in); their spread is usually about 30cm (12in). P.barbatus (often offered as Chelone barbata) is usually 100cm (3¼ ft) tall with a spread of 40cm (16in). They are tolerant of any soil type but should be protected in winter with a mulch of peat or bracken litter. Take a few cuttings in September and overwinter them in a coldframe just in case. Among the hardier cultivars of P.hartwegii are 'Cherry Ripe', 'Firebird' and 'Garnet' all in shades of red.

 6–8 ○ ●

SUMMER

Philadelphus Hybrids

'Belle Etoile'

'Virginal'

Mock Orange Blossom (often mistakenly referred to as Syringa) is an invaluable flowering shrub, growing readily on any soil type in sun or light shade and giving a bravura display of sweet-smelling pure white flowers throughout June and July. The flowering stems must be pruned back to within a couple of centimetres of the old wood as soon as the blossom has faded. On average they will attain a height of between 1.5m and 2.5m (5—16ft) with a spread of between 1m and 2m (3¼—6½ft). Cultivars include 'Belle Etoile' with large single flowers flushed with pink at the base, 'Virginal' with huge clusters of double flowers, and *P.coronarius* 'Aureus' which has bright golden juvenile foliage.

🌼 6–7 ◑ ◗◗

Phlox maculata and *Phlox paniculata*

P.paniculata 'Prince of Orange'

These stately North American perennials with their various shades of white, pink and purple provide a striking feature in the centre of a border. They demand a well-drained position in sun or light shade, with rich soil containing plenty of humus. A spring mulch of compost or leafmould is always beneficial. *P.maculata* cultivars grow to about 90cm (36in) tall with a spread of up to 60cm (24in). *P.paniculata* cultivars usually attain similar dimensions but there are also dwarf forms such as 'Pinafore Pink' which will reach only 45cm (18in) tall by 25cm (10in) across. All flower profusely from July to late August.

🌼 7–8 ◑ ◗◗

SUMMER

Phormium tenax

'Purpureum'

The **New Zealand Flax** is a striking foliage plant which will settle readily on any soil type in sun or semi-shade. The clump of sword-like leaves can stand anything up to 2m (6½ ft) tall by 1m (3¼ ft) across according to cultivar. Many have interesting variegations such as the pink and bronze 'Maori Sunrise' (100cm/3¼ ft tall by 80cm/2¾ ft across) or the green and golden 'Yellow Wave' (70cm/28in tall by 40cm/16in across). In July or August the flower spikes emerge from the centre of the clump, standing usually two or three times the height of the foliage so that a tall-growing cultivar such as 'Purpureum' (2m/6½ ft tall and 1m/3¼ ft across) will produce a flower spike between 4m and 5m (13–16ft) tall.

🌺 7–8 ◗ ♦♦

Phygelius capensis

'Coccineus'

The **Cape Figwort** is a delightful small South African shrub which thrives against a sheltered, south-facing wall or in a sunny well-drained spot at the front of a border. It is tolerant of any soil type and, if grown as a free-standing shrub, will attain a height of about 150cm (5ft) with a spread of 100cm (3¼ ft), but against a wall it could easily grow to twice that size. It requires no pruning apart from the removal of dead wood or weak shoots in April. The clone *P.capensis* 'Coccineus' is the one usually offered and has bright scarlet, trumpet-shaped flowers from July to September. *P.aequalis* is also occasionally offered, but is less hardy.

🌺 7–9 ○ ♦

SUMMER

Polygonum affine and *Polygonum bistorta* 'Superbum'

P.affine 'Donald Lowndes'

Many **Knotweeds** are too rampantly invasive for the average garden but it is possible to obtain reasonably well-behaved cultivars of these attractive herbaceous perennials that will give good, weed-suppressing ground cover and a rich display of flowers for most of the summer. *P.affine* cultivars such as 'Darjeeling Red' and 'Donald Lowndes' make a spreading clump about 25cm (10in) tall and up to 60cm (24in) across, while the soft pink *P.bistorta* 'Superbum' (**Snakeweed**) stands about 90cm (36in) tall with a spread of 50cm (20in). They can be increased by division in spring if required.

 7–10 ◐ ♦♦♦

Polygonum baldschuanicum

The **Russian Vine** is often nicknamed the Mile-a-Minute plant with very good reason, for this rampant climber is capable of extending up to 6m (20ft) in one season. Mercifully it will stand hard pruning in the spring and a second trim in late summer to keep it in bounds. It tolerates any soil and any aspect, although the huge clusters of tiny creamy-white flowers, faintly flushed with pink, are borne more profusely by a plant in full sun. It flowers from June until early autumn. If you are training it up a chain-link fence or trellis you must make quite sure that it is well supported, otherwise the sheer weight of flowers and foliage could make it collapse.

P.baldschuanicum

  6–9 ◐ ♦♦

Potentilla astrosanguinea and *Potentilla nepalensis*

These herbaceous **Potentillas** are attractive, low-growing plants for the front of the border. *P.astrosanguinea* cultivars vary in colour from the yellow 'William Robinson' to the pillar-box red 'Gibson's Scarlet', while *P.nepalensis* cultivars include the soft pink 'Miss Wilmot' and the multi-coloured 'Roxana'. Their height is usually about 45cm (18in) with a spread of 50cm (20in) and they will succeed in any well-drained soil in sun or light shade. They flower from June to late August and their bright green, strawberry-like foliage is also very attractive. Plants can be increased by division in March or April.

P.astrosanguinea 'Gibson's Scarlet'

Potentilla fruticosa

'Elizabeth'

This shrubby **Potentilla** is greatly valued for its long flowering season. It is tolerant of any soil type and flourishes equally well in sun or light shade. The flower colours range mostly from pale yellow to golden-orange, with the primrose coloured 'Katherine Dykes' and the canary-yellow 'Elizabeth' among the favourites. Height will vary according to cultivar, from the 45cm (18in) tall 'Tilford Cream' which spreads to about 60cm (24in), to the 75cm (30in) tall 'Gold Finger' which has a spread of 100cm (39in). 'Katherine Dykes', however, is usually much taller, attaining up to 2m (6½ft) tall by 1m (3¼ft) across. Light pruning in March will keep the bush compact and shapely.

Prunella webbiana

'Loveliness'

Self-Heal is a useful ground-covering herbaceous perennial for sun or light shade. It thrives in any fertile garden soil but will not survive severe drought. In flower it stands about 25cm (10in) tall and one plant will have a spread of up to 40cm (16in), but once a group is established it will spread itself by seed and could rapidly cover several square metres unless kept in check. Colours range from the pure white 'Alba' and the soft pink 'Pink Loveliness' to the pale mauve 'Loveliness'. All flower in June and July and the flowering period can be maximized by nipping off dead flower spikes as soon as their blossoms have faded.

  6–7

Ranunculus acris **'Flore Pleno'**

Yellow **Bachelor's Buttons** provide a vivid patch of bright golden flowers in May, June and July and thrive on any moist garden soil in sun or light shade. They are a close relative of the common buttercup but nowhere near so invasive. In flower the wiry stems bearing pretty double flowers stand about 60cm (24in) tall above a 40cm (16in) wide mound of bright green foliage. They can be increased by dividing the clumps in spring just as the leaves are unfolding and a good mulch of compost or leafmould in March is also beneficial. If necessary, support with stakes and retaining wires.

 5–7

'Flore Pleno'

SUMMER

Rheum palmatum

R. palmatum

Sorrel Rhubarb is a native of China and Tibet and a most intriguing plant to watch as it emerges in late spring, unfolding its foliage in May from huge, brilliant red buds into hand-shaped leaves which are often at least 30cm (12in) across. It will form a clump about 80cm (2¾ft) tall and 100cm (3¼ft) across. The spikes of creamy-white flowers that emerge in late May and bloom throughout June are about 200cm (6½ft) tall. All in all this is a magnificently statuesque herbaceous perennial for deep, moist, partially shaded sites, and it looks particularly striking at the edge of a pond or stream. The cultivar 'Atropurpurea' has especially beautiful juvenile foliage.

🌼 6 ◑ 💧💧💧

Rodgersia pinnata

'Superba'

This is an imposing herbaceous perennial for a semi-shaded position on rich, well-cultivated, moist soil. It will grow much more vigorously if a substantial amount of well-rotted leafmould or compost is dug into the site before planting. The best times to plant are either early November or late March. The dark green or bronze foliage forms a clump about 80cm (2¾ft) across and, in flower, the plant stands 90cm (3ft) tall. The cultivar 'Superba' has bronzy-purple leaves and plumes of soft pink flowers and is widely offered. 'Elegans' with its sweetly scented creamy-white flowers and green foliage is harder to obtain but well worth snapping up if you see it offered.

🌼 7–8 ◑ 💧💧💧

SUMMER

'Norman Hartnell'

'Blue Moon'

'Mountbatten'

Roses

The choice of roses offered nowadays is vast. Apart from the modern cultivars, which are usually divided into Large Flowered (Hybrid Tea) and Cluster Roses (Floribunda), it is now much easier to obtain a good representation of Species and Old Fashioned Roses as well as an interesting range of Modern Shrub Roses.

Large Flowered and Cluster Roses

The choice of cultivars within this group is very wide indeed. Container-grown specimens can be planted at any time of the year but care should be taken not to disturb the rootball too much when transferring from the container to the planting position. Plants purchased with bare roots should be planted in later autumn or early spring. In either case, the bed should have been well dug over beforehand, but refrain from adding too much manure or fertilizer. Any broken or damaged shoots should be carefully pruned off before planting.

Large Flowered and Cluster Roses usually make substantial bushes but the labels almost always simply say 'short', 'medium' or 'tall'. As a general rule you can assume 'short' to mean not more than 60cm (24in) tall with a spread of 40cm (16in), 'medium' to mean anything between 60cm and 90cm (2–3ft) tall with a spread of not more than 70cm (2¼ ft), and 'tall' to mean anything from 90cm to 200cm (3–6½ ft) tall and spreading up to 150 cm (5ft). All roses of this type

SUMMER

'Peace'

'Iceberg'

flower on their new wood and therefore require careful pruning in early spring to promote plenty of growth.

There are any number of reasons for choosing a rose and it can be fun to go for something more than just the colour. Followers of haute couture can plant 'Chanelle', 'Christian Dior' or 'Norman Hartnell'.

Some people prefer to collect scented cultivars such as 'Margaret Merril', a soft pink-and-white Cluster Rose with a superb perfume or 'Blue Moon','Mountbatten', Chinatown', or 'Fragrant Cloud'.

There is a particular group of cultivars which is long-lived, disease-resistant, unfussy as to soil type and gives long, brilliant displays of bloom with the minimum of attention. 'Peace' is one such old favourite, along with 'Queen Elizabeth','Iceberg' and the rich salmon-coloured 'Elizabeth of Glamis'.

Roses always make a welcome gift and it is now possible to obtain both 'Silver Wedding' and 'Ruby Wedding'. 'Dearest', 'My Choice', 'My Love' and 'Congratulations' make charming presents for all sorts of celebrations.

There are numerous climbing cultivars They are usually divided into Summer Flowering and Repeat Flowering cultivars and are best pruned in early winter, keeping the main framework but removing any weak or badly placed shoots and cutting back the current year's growth to within five or six buds from the old wood. Of the Repeat Flowering cultivars, 'Handel' is deservedly popular, but 'Bantry Bay' or the sweetly

'My Choice'

'Danse du Feu'

'Chelsea Pensioner'

'Graham Thomas'

scented, salmon-flowered 'Compassion' are also widely planted. The bright red 'Danse du Feu' and the rich creamy-yellow 'Golden Showers' will do well against an open north- or east-facing wall.

There are also a great many miniatures offered nowadays which make a delightful edging to the front of a formal rose bed or alongside a path in full sun. The dainty little 'Easter Morning' or the bright scarlet 'Chelsea Pensioner' and others like them usually grow to about 50cm (20in) tall with a spread of 30cm (12in) and require the same treatment as their larger brothers and sisters.

Species, Old Fashioned and Modern Shrub Roses

This broad group of flowering shrub roses looks particularly attractive in herbaceous or shrub borders, scrambling through trees or trained over broad, sunny walls or spreading prostrate on unmowable banks.They come in all shapes and sizes, from a dainty 60cm (24in) across by 60cm tall to the huge, handsome Ramblers that will rapidly scramble 5m (16ft) or 10m (33ft) into a tree making a canopy of blossom up to 6m (20ft) across.

In recent years there has been a revival of hybridization giving new cultivars such as 'Graham Thomas' and 'Sadler's Wells'.

Among the old Centifolia Roses, which have flattened, cabbage-shaped, richly scented flowers,'Fantin-Latour' is deservedly popular, producing a stunning display in June and July. Apart from cutting out

SUMMER

'Sadler's Wells'

'Fantin-Latour'

'Dr Van Fleet'

'Lady Penzance'

dead wood or weak shoots in autumn, Centifolia Roses need to be pruned back into shape only if they become straggly or unkempt or congested in the centre.

If you have an old fruit tree which could support a Rambling Rose there are a number of specimens for you to choose from. 'Dr Van Fleet' will attain about 6m (20ft) and give a rich summer display of fragrant, flesh-pink double flowers. 'Wedding Day' is a very vigorous climber reaching 10m (33ft) or more and it tolerates poor soils. *Rosa filipes* 'Kiftsgate' is probably the most rampant of all and is tolerant of quite deep shade, making it an excellent subject for larger trees. Its fragrant, creamy-white flowers are followed by a brilliantly coloured array of heps in the autumn. On no account should it be planted in a confined corner or its vigorous strangling habit will soon make it a thorough nuisance. The ever-popular 'Albertine', with its sweetly scented, coppery-pink double flowers, is probably the most widely planted hybrid of *Rosa wichuraiana* which is the main species parent of so many modern Rambling Roses. It attains a height of between 6m and 7m (20—23ft) and grows equally well against a wall, trained over a pergola or rambling up a tree or trelliswork. Apart from the removal of dead or inconveniently placed shoots and branches, Rambling Roses require no regular pruning.

The Penzance Hybrid Sweet Briars are particularly good for a medium-height hedge — say 2m (6½ft) tall and 150cm (5ft)

'Salet'

'Mme Isaac Pereire'

'Baron Girod de l'Ain'

wide. Both 'Lord Penzance' and 'Lady Penzance' form a dense, vigorous bush, well furnished right down to the ground.

Moss Roses are usually as sweet-smelling as their close relatives, the Centifolia or Cabbage Roses, but are less coarse and sprawling in habit. Most cultivars, such as 'Common Moss' (sometimes offered as 'Old Pink Moss') and 'Comtesse de Murinais', are only Summer Flowering but a few, like the dainty little 'Ma Ponctuee' and the superbly scented 'Salet', are repeat flowering.

Most Bourbon Roses, such as 'Louise Odier' and 'Mme Pierre Oger', make a bush about 150cm (5ft) tall by 90cm (3ft) across but some others, such as 'Mme Isaac Pereire', grow up to 2.5m (8ft) tall and are best if given the support of a wall or high fence. Hybrid Perpetual Roses, such as the rich deep crimson 'Baron de Bonstettin' and the white-edged, brilliant red 'Baron Girod de l'Ain' form dense, vigorous bushes up to 140cm (4½ft) tall and 90cm (3ft) across with fragrant blossoms ideal for cutting for indoor decoration.

The ancient race of Alba Roses, many of which date back to the Middle Ages, the elegantly graceful Damask and Portland Roses, the old China Roses which prove too tender for many gardens and the dainty, sweet-smelling Hybrid Musk Roses are also readily available and well worth considering.

Rudbeckia laciniata

'Goldquelle'

This species of **Coneflower** is a relative of the annual Black-eyed Susan. Some cultivars can grow as tall as 2m (6½ft) and make an attractive display at the back of the border from August to early October. They thrive on any fertile garden soil in sun or light shade, and the incorporation of some well-rotted manure or compost before planting is beneficial, as is a spring mulch of the same each year. Because of their height they must be supported with stakes. The flowering period will be extended if dead flowers are removed as soon as they fade. 'Goldquelle' is a compact form growing only 70cm (28in) tall with a spread of 40cm (16in), but 'Golden Glow' will reach 2m (6½ft) in height and spread 1m (3¼ft) across.

   8–10 ○ ◗◗

Ruta graveolens

'Jackman's Blue'

Rue, also known as **Herb of Grace**, displays clusters of small yellow flowers in June and July but is primarily grown for its beautiful blue-green foliage. It is a semi-evergreen sub-shrub and thrives in a sunny or lightly shaded position on any light, well-drained soil. To ensure a compact bushy shape it should be pruned back in early spring, removing any over-elongated or weak shoots. The foliage has a bitter acrid smell when bruised. 'Jackman's Blue' is commonly acknowledged to be the best form; it will make a neat bush about 100cm (3¼ft) tall and 100cm across within five years. It is an excellent plant for a low hedge.

  6–7 ◑ ◆◆◆

Salvia officinalis

'Tricolor'

Common Sage is not only a very useful culinary herb but is also an attractive, semi-evergreen garden shrub in its own right. As well as the ordinary soft, grey-green leafed form there is a handsome purple leafed cultivar 'Purpurescens'; a green and gold variegated cultivar 'Icterina'; and a lovely white, pink, purple and green-leafed cultivar 'Tricolor'. The foliage is pungently fragrant whatever its colour and they all flower in June. They grow to about 70cm (28in) tall and 80cm (33in) across and thrive best in full sun on light, well-drained soil but can be grown in partial shade if they are pruned each spring.

 6

Salvia × superba

'May Night'

This handsome herbaceous **Sage** is a most attractive purple flowered, medium-height plant for the centre of the border and many of the cultivars available bloom continuously throughout the summer. They succeed easily in sun or light shade on any well-drained, fertile garden soil and can be divided or transplanted in spring or autumn. S. × *superba* itself will attain 100cm (3¼ ft) in height with a spread of 40cm (16in) and the unusual pink flowered cultivar 'Rose Queen' stands 75cm (30in) tall with a spread of 30cm (12in). 'May Night' is one of the shorter cultivars at only 45cm (18in) tall and 30cm (12in) across and blooms early in the summer, while 'East Friesland' is of a similar size but flowers longer.

 5–7

Santolina chamaecyparissus

S.chamaecyparissus

The **Cotton Lavender** is also frequently offered under the name *Santolina incana*, and its common name is often given the other way round as **Lavender Cotton**. Its evergreen foliage makes a low mound, rarely more than 50cm (20in) tall by 80cm (33in) across and is bright green in winter, turning grey as the summer arrives. The lemon-yellow flowers stand well clear of the leaves on tall slim stalks throughout July. The shrub requires a sunny position on light, free-draining soil and should be lightly trimmed in spring. A smaller-growing form, 'Nana', never grows more than 30cm (12in) tall with a spread of 50cm (20in).

 7

Saponaria ocymoides

S.ocymoides

Rock Soapwort is a pretty little rock-garden perennial which does best in full sun on well-drained, sandy soil. Even in flower it stands less than 15cm (6in) tall but will gradually spread to form a broad, ground-hugging mat of foliage about 50cm (20in) across. Its main flowering period is early June but it will continue to bloom intermittently until the end of July or even early August. The bright pink flowers make an attractive splash of colour on a rock garden or spilling over the edge of a low retaining wall at the front of a raised bed. The cultivar 'Rubra Compacta' is a rich dark pink while the ordinary *S.ocymoides* is a softer shell-pink.

 6–8

SUMMER

Saponaria officinalis

'Rosea Plena'

The **Common Soapwort** is a familiar native British wildflower in many hedgerows and woodlands, but a number of double flowered forms have become established as popular garden perennials. The pink 'Rosea Plena', the dark red 'Rubra Plena' and the white 'Alba Plena' all make good, easily grown plants about 70cm (28in) tall with a spread of up to 60cm (24in). They tolerate any soil type provided that it is well drained and will thrive equally well in sun or light shade. All cultivars flower from August until the first frost of autumn, but they have a vigorous and invasive nature and should not be grown beside perennials with a less robust constitution.

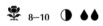 8–10 ◐ ◆◆

Scabiosa caucasica

'Clive Greaves'

The frilly-edged pincushion flowers of the **Perennial Scabious** appear a few at a time from the end of June until early October. They require a sunny position in well-drained chalky soil; if your garden soil is neutral then work in a good helping of lime before planting, but if your garden soil is acid the plant will not thrive whatever you do for it. The flower colours range from the deep violet 'Imperial Purple' through the light mauve 'Clive Greaves' and the soft blue 'Loddon Anna' to the creamy-white 'Miss Wilmott' and 'Bressingham White'. All stand up to 90cm (36in) tall and spread about 45cm (18in) and are easily propagated by dividing the clumps in spring.

 6–9 ○ ◆

SUMMER

Sedum spathufolium and *Sedum spurium*

S.spathufolium 'Capablanca'

S.spurium

Stonecrops form attractive cushions of succulent foliage which remain interesting all year round. These two species are much less invasive than their close relative *S.acre*, and far more suitable for most gardens. *S.spathufolium* has rosettes of silvery-grey or purple foliage on short stems which even in flower are never more than 10cm (4in) high. An established plant will have a spread of about 35cm (14in). The foliage of 'Capablanca' is silver while that of 'Purpureum' is dark wine-red, and both have bright golden flowers in June and July. *S.spurium* is the same size but its flowers are bright pink. Both species require a sunny, well-drained site.

 6–7 ○ ◆

Senecio greyii

S.greyii

The soft, silver-grey felted foliage of this attractive evergreen shrub provides an elegant contrast to the many bright colours of the summer border. In July and August it puts up sprays of golden daisy-like flowers but is mainly grown for the beauty of its leaves. It rarely grows more than 90cm (3ft) tall but could achieve a sideways spread of up to 2m (6½ft). It grows best on free-draining soil in full sun. It is quite unaffected by coastal winds, making it an excellent seaside shrub. It will probably need pruning in early spring to remove straggly shoots and maintain a neat dense shape.

 7–8 ○ ◆

Sidalcea malvaeflora

'Elsie Hough'

The **Prairie Mallow** makes an attractive medium-height perennial for the centre of the border. It grows well in any fertile garden soil and flowers equally readily in sun or light shade. Height varies from 70cm to 120cm (28—48in) according to cultivar and the spread is usually about 40cm (16in). Older cultivars such as the light pink 'Elsie Hough', the rosy-pink 'Rose Queen', and the warm salmon-pink 'William Smith' stand over 100cm (3¼ ft) tall, while the more modern cultivars such as 'Croftway Red' and the shell-pink 'Loveliness' average about 80cm (2¾ ft). All bloom from July to September and the flower spikes should be cut out as soon as the flowers have faded.

  7—9 ◑ ♦♦

Sisyrinchium striatum

The **Satin Flower** is a member of the Iris family and, indeed, until the flower spikes emerge you could be forgiven for mistaking it for just another iris. The foliage forms a clump about 30cm (12in) tall and 40cm (16in) across when well established, and in June and July the elegant 70cm (28in) tall stems of creamy-white flowers form an early summer feature in the herbaceous border. They are quite at home in any soil type provided that it is well drained, and do best in a hot, dry, sunny position. Every three or four years the clump should be divided and replanted to prevent it from becoming too congested.

 6—7 ○ ♦

S.striatum

SUMMER

Solanum crispum

S.crispum

The **Chilean Potato Tree** needs the support of a warm south- or west-facing wall or fence and, if carefully secured, will rapidly attain a height of up to 5m (16ft) and a spread of 4m (13ft) although wind and frost damage will keep it smaller in cold or exposed areas. The semi-evergreen shrub produces clusters of purple-blue flowers with golden centres from July to September, and the clone 'Glasnevin' often flowers until October. Although the main framework is woody, the flowering shoots are herbaceous in habit and should be pruned out in late autumn. It will usually shoot again even if severely damaged by frost.

 7–9

Solidalgo canadensis

'Goldenmosa'

Golden Rod has long been a favourite late-flowering herbaceous perennial, but its habit of falling over if it was not supported with stakes often caused frustration. Thankfully, modern cultivars are mostly shorter and much more sturdy, so these problems seldom arise nowadays. All thrive in any ordinary garden soil in a sunny position and display their bright golden plumes of flowers from August to October. 'Golden Thumb' is a dwarf, attaining only 30cm (12in) tall with a spread of 25cm (10in), while 'Crown of Rays' is about 45cm (18in) tall by 30cm (12in) across. 'Goldenmosa' and 'Lenore' are both 75cm (30in) tall and 40cm (16in) across, while 'Mimosa' and 'Golden Wings' stand over 150cm (5ft) tall and 60cm (2ft) across.

 7–9

Spartium junceum

S.junceum

Spanish Broom is a vigorous, graceful shrub which does well in an open, sunny, well-drained position. It is tolerant of any soil type and flowers from July until early autumn. If left unchecked it will make a gaunt, sprawling shrub up to 3m (10ft) tall and at least 2m (6½ ft) across, but it is best to prune out the flowering shoots in September as soon as the blossom has faded, keeping it to a height of about 2m (6½ ft) and a spread of 1m (3¼ ft), taking care not to cut into the old wood. The brilliant golden honey-scented flowers make this a great favourite for small sheltered gardens or a sunny spot outside a living-room window.

 7–9 ○

Spiraea japonica

Some cultivars of S.japonica are occasionally offered as S. × bumalda, but they all have the same habit and require the same treatment. They form low, dome-shaped shrubs, usually between 60cm and 90cm (24–36in) tall and are as broad as they are high. The flower colours are usually various shades of pink or red, but white cultivars such as 'Snowmound' are sometimes available. They grow easily in any fertile garden soil and flower best in an open sunny position. Since they flower in July and August on their new season's growth, they need to be pruned back hard in March. The bright crimson 'Anthony Waterer' is one of the taller cultivars and has occasional variegated leaves.

'Anthony Waterer'

 7–8 ○

SUMMER

Stachys lanata

S. lanata

Lambs' Ears is a most attractive ground-covering perennial with soft, silver-grey felt-like foliage and spikes of pinkish-purple flowers. It thrives on any ordinary, well-drained garden soil in sun or light shade. When in flower in June and July it stands about 30cm (12in) tall with a spread of anything up to 100cm (3¼ ft) or more because the stems put down roots as they go along. It can be quite invasive if not kept in check. There is a cultivar called 'Silver Carpet' which normally does not flower but simply makes a spreading mat of foliage 4cm (1¾ in) high. 'Sheila MacQueen' has larger leaves and taller flower spikes than the simple species.

 6-7

Stokesia laevis

S. laevis

The cornflower-like blooms of **Stokes' Aster** begin to open in July and the plant will continue to flower until the first frosts of autumn. It is an attractive and undemanding herbaceous perennial for the front of the border, standing up to 45cm (18in) tall with a spread of 30cm (12in), and it thrives in any moist, fertile garden soil in sun or light shade. The flowers are usually various shades of blue from the pale blue 'Blue Star' to the deep lavender 'Superba', but there is also a white cultivar 'Alba'. The crown may suffer frost damage in severe weather and an autumn mulch of bracken litter or peat is a wise precaution.

 6-9

SUMMER

Tamarix pentandra

This species is a much better garden plant than the common **Tamarisk** (*T.gallica*), and will form a medium-sized shrub up to 3m (10ft) tall by 2m (6½ft) across within ten years. It requires a sunny position on moist, fertile soil and is only slightly lime-tolerant; on very chalky soils it simply won't survive. The sweet-smelling, pale pink flowers appear in August on the current year's growth and the shrub must be pruned back to within two or three buds of the old wood every March. The clone 'Rubra' has much darker pink flowers than the type but the same feathery, silver-grey foliage.

T. pentandra

 8 ○ ♦♦

Thalictrum aquilegifolium and Thalictrum dipterocarpum

These two species of **Meadow Rue** make graceful perennials for the herbaceous border. *T.aquilegifolium* flowers from May to July and is the shorter of the two, seldom attaining more than 100cm (3¼ft) tall with a spread of 40cm (16in). Most of its cultivars have mauve or purple flowers, and 'Thundercloud' is a particularly handsome deep lilac. There is also a white cultivar, 'Album', but this is not so frequently offered. Some cultivars of *T.dipterocarpum* can grow as tall as 180cm (6ft) with a spread of 60cm (24in) and usually need the support of stakes, but 'Hewitt's Double' with its attractive mauve flowers attains only half that size. Both species thrive in any moist garden soil in sun or semi-shade.

T. aquilegifolium

T. dipterocarpum

 5-7 ◑ ♦♦

SUMMER

Thymus citriodorus and *Thymus vulgaris*

T. citriodorus 'Aureus'

T. vulgaris

Lemon Thyme and **Common Thyme** both make attractive dwarf shrubs for the rock garden or the front of a border. The lemon thyme, *T.citriodorus*, usually has dark green foliage but there is a golden-leafed cultivar 'Aureus' and sometimes a variegated cultivar 'Silver Posie' can be obtained. All give the characteristic warm lemon scent when a leaf is squeezed. Common thyme, *T.vulgaris*, being evergreen, will oblige with a supply of foliage all year round. Both species grow to about 25cm (10in) tall and 30cm (12in) across and thrive best on poor, dry soil in full sun. Their sweetly scented mauve flowers appear in May and June.

🌹 5-6 ○ ◗

Tiarella cordifolia and *Tiarella polyphylla*

T. cordifolia

The **Foam Flower** is tolerant of all soils and makes a marvellous evergreen herbaceous plant for ground cover in moist semi-shaded places. The foliage of *T.cordifolia* grows to a height of about 20cm (8in) and from May to August the 40cm (16in) tall spikes of ivory-white flowers make a most pleasing effect. *T.polyphylla* is about 30cm (12in) high, the flowers stand about 60cm (24in) tall and it blooms at the same time. The spread of an individual plant of either species is usually about 40cm (16in), but *T.cordifolia* is a slightly more rampant spreader.Clumps can be divided and replanted in March if required.

🌹 5-8 ● ◗◗

SUMMER

Tradescantia virginiana

'Isis'

The **Spiderwort** is available with flowers in many shades of pink or blue, and there are good white cultivars also. They are tolerant of all soils but grow best in a moist position in partial shade. Their usual height is between 50cm and 60cm (20—24in) with a spread of about 40cm (16in). The sword-shaped leaves are often attacked by slugs as they emerge in spring, and a carefully positioned slug-trap will help to get them away to a good start. They begin flowering in June and will continue to open new blooms right through the summer. The most commonly offered cultivars are 'Osprey' which is pure white, 'Purple Dome', the deep blue 'Isis' and the neat growing 'Carmine Glow'

 6—9

Trollius europaeus

'Orange Princess'

Globe Flowers make a brilliant splash of yellow in early summer and thrive on any moist soil in sun or light shade. If your soil is fairly free-draining, then you should incorporate plenty of moisture-retaining humus such as compost or peat before planting. The usual flowering period is May and June, but the clear yellow 'Earliest of All' earns its name by opening its first flowers in April. Their usual height is between 60cm and 75cm (24—30in) with a spread of 40cm (16in), and the flower colours range from the pale primrose 'Alabaster' and the lemon-yellow 'Canary Bird' to the bright golden-orange 'Orange Princess' and 'Commander in Chief'.

 5—6

163

SUMMER

Verbascum hybridum

'Gainsborough'

Mulleins thrive best on poor, free-draining, chalky soils in an open sunny position. In soil that is too rich they will flower only sparsely and could well die at the end of their first season. In suitable conditions they make a broad rosette of furry grey-green leaves about 40cm (16in) across and 10cm (4in) high and in July and August send up 100cm to 130cm (3¼ −4¼ ft) tall spikes of flowers. Most of the cultivars have flowers in shades of yellow from the pale lemon 'Gainsborough' to the rich apricot 'Cotswold Queen' and the deep gold 'C.L.Adams', but there are pink cultivars such as the deep rose 'Pink Domino' and white cultivars such as 'Mont Blanc' or the statuesque 200cm (6½ ft) tall 'Miss Willmott'.

🌼 7-8 ○ 💧💧

Veronica

V. spicata

V. teucrium

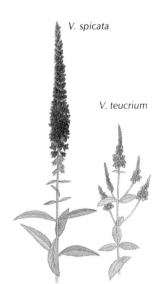

There are several species of **Speedwell** offered and all thrive on any well-drained garden soil in sun or light shade. *V.gentianoides* is an attractive pale blue, early-flowering species that grows about 60cm (24in) tall with a spread of 30cm (12in) and blooms from late April until June. The grey-leafed *V.incana* is normally 35cm (14in) tall with a spread of 25cm (10in) and has deep blue flowers from June to August. *V.spicata* forms a mass of deep-green foliage 30cm (12in) across and sends up 45cm (18in) tall spikes of flowers from August to September. Apart from the usual blue cultivars of *V.spicata*, there are also pink and white ones.

🌼 4-6 or 8-10 ◑ 💧💧

164

SUMMER

Viburnum opulus and Viburnum plicatum

V. opulus 'Sterile'

V. plicatum 'Lanarth'

The **Guelder Rose** and the
Japanese Snowball are popular
medium-sized shrubs. In both
cases the sterile forms give the
most prolific blossom.
V.plicatum 'Grandiflorum'
blooms first, commencing in
late May through to early July,
while *V.opulus* 'Sterile' (the
SnowballTree) opens its flowers
in late June and continues to
August. They are tolerant of all
soils and do best in a moist site
in partial shade. *V.opulus* will
make a broad, bushy shrub up to
3m (10ft) tall by 2.5m (8ft)
across, while *V.plicatum* has a
more upright habit, growing to
2.5m (8ft) tall by 1.75m (5¾ft)
across. Neither requires any
pruning except to remove dead
wood in March.

 5-7 ● ▲▲▲

Vinca minor

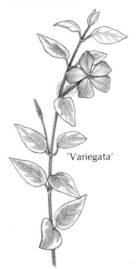

'Variegata'

The **Lesser Periwinkle** flowers in
May and June, a little later than
V.major. It makes excellent
ground cover in sun or shade
and is completely unfussy as to
soil type. The plant usually
stands about 10cm (4in) tall
with an initial spread of up to
20cm (8in), but its trailing shoots
root at the tips and form new
plants so it can rapidly spread
itself over 3 to 4 sq.m
(34—43 sq.ft). The flowers are
either white or blue and there is
a wide diversity of foliage
colours. 'Bowles Variety' has
larger flowers of a true
periwinkle-blue and is neater in
habit than most. 'Gertrude
Jekyll' is the most free flowering
white-flowered cultivar but is
not always so easily obtainable.

 5-6 ● ▲▲

SUMMER

Viola and *Violetta*

Viola 'Arkwright Beauty'

Violetta 'Rebecca'

Once established, these small-flowered relatives of the pansy will form spreading mats of bloom up to 30cm (12in) across for the whole of the summer. **Violas** like the purple 'Prince Henry' and the yellow 'Prince John' will spread rapidly by seeding themselves around, but **Violettas** are best propagated by cuttings. Violettas grow well underneath roses or in moist shady corners and should be sprayed regularly against greenfly. Their new growth in spring is often decimated by slugs and a slug trap filled with beer will protect them until they begin to flower. Regular dead-heading and an occasional liquid feed will encourage flowers all summer long.

 5-9

Weigela florida and *Weigela hybrida*

W. *florida* 'Variegata

W. *hybrida* 'Bristol Ruby'

These handsome shrubs make a bold display of pink or red blossoms each June and, since they flower on one-year-old wood, must be pruned back to within 3cm or 4cm (1¼–1¾ in) of the old wood as soon as the flowers have faded. W. *florida* makes a dense bush about 150cm (5ft) tall and 100cm (3¼ ft) broad, but W. *hybrida* cultivars are more open and will attain a summer flowering size of 200cm (6¼ ft) tall by 150cm (5ft) broad within eight or nine years. The most popular cultivar of W. *florida* is 'Variegata', while of the W. *hybrida* cultivars 'Bristol Ruby' and 'Abel Carriere' are among the most frequently offered. All require a moist site in semi-shade.

 6

SUMMER

Yucca filamentosa and Yucca gloriosa

Y. filamentosa 'Variegata'

These two sub-shrubs are fairly similar in appearance when young, but Y.filamentosa remains stemless, forming a broad clump 80cm (2¾ ft) tall and up to 100cm (3¼ ft) across while Y.gloriosa grows its crown of sword-shaped leaves from a short, thick trunk and will eventually make a specimen about 250cm (8ft) tall and 150cm (5ft) broad. The tips of the leaves are often dangerously sharp. In spite of their exotic sub-tropical appearance they are hardy, but require a hot, dry position on free-draining soil. The huge spikes of creamy-white bell-shaped flowers are borne in July and August and both species have a variegated cultivar as well as the green-leafed form.

 7-8 ◯ ◗

Zantedeschia aethiopica

'Crowborough'

The white **Arum Lily** is a slightly tender perennial suited to very moist, rich soil at the margin of a pond or stream. It requires generous feeding and the best method is to mulch it heavily with well-rotted compost in autumn so that the crown is protected from winter frost. 'Crowborough' is a particularly fine form with elegant white flower spathes appearing from August until early October. Its handsome, glossy green foliage which begins unfolding in May is also attractive in its own right. The plant will grow to about 90cm (3ft) tall with a spread of up to 80cm (2¾ ft). Clumps can be divided in spring as they start into growth if extra plants are required.

 8-9 ● ♦♦♦

AUTUMN

As the flowers of summer fade, the brilliantly-coloured berries and glorious autumn foliage of trees and shrubs become the predominant feature in the garden. If your soil is chalky you must choose autumn foliage plants with care because many deciduous trees and shrubs give a poor display on alkaline soils. The brilliant autumn red of *Acer rubrum*, for instance, becomes a rather muddy yellow on chalky soils, but *Prunus sargentii* will perform magnificently. Berry-bearing shrubs sometimes require the prescence of a male pollinator and so care should be taken when selecting to ascertain whether the plant is monoecious (having male and female flowers separate but on the same plant), dioecious (having male and female flowers on different plants) or bisexual (having the male and female organs within the same flower). Usually one male plant of a dioecious species, properly sited, is enough to pollinate all the females within an average-sized garden. Late-flowering perennials such as chrysanthemums and michaelmas daisies should be supported with stakes against autumn gales. New bulbs for next spring will be on sale at this time so this is the moment to add to your collection — it is surprising how the addition of a few new bulbs each year gradually builds up into a sizeable display. By noting what you already have, the flowering period can be extended by the purchase of species or cultivars that flower earlier or later than those already in your garden.

Abelia × grandiflora

A. × grandiflora

This slightly tender medium-sized shrub is best grown against a sunny wall and in mild areas is often semi-evergreen. In autumn its display of pale pink or white flowers on elegant arching branches is most attractive. Although less fragrant than its parent *A. chinensis*, it has a pleasing perfume. Being hardier and more vigorous, it makes a better garden shrub attaining a height of 3m (10ft) or more and a spread of about 2m (6½ft). Prune only to remove dead wood or to maintain a neat, well-balanced shape. Not a plant for very exposed situations, but in the right spot its bright green foliage makes a pleasing background for border plants.

 10–11 ○ ◆◆

Acer rubrum

A. rubrum

The **Red Maple** is a close relative of the sugar maple but is faster growing and turns colour earlier in the autumn. It is a good choice for a specimen tree in a medium or large garden where its handsome silhouette offers year-round interest. Within twenty years it can attain a height of 12m (40ft) and, with careful training in its early stages, a clear trunk of about 3m (10ft) making it suitable for planting near a boundary wall or in a lawn. The magnificent scarlet autumn foliage is most brilliant on acid soil; it really does not perform properly where there is a lot of lime present. City conditions are no problem provided it gets plenty of moisture.

 ◑ ◆◆◆

Achillea filipendulina

The **Fernleaf Yarrow** is a useful plant for the centre or back of an herbaceous border, growing up to 150cm (5ft) high. In windy situations it should be supported with stakes. The attractive clumps of feathery, grey-green foliage appear early in the year giving some cover to otherwise bare borders. The plate-like flowerheads sometimes open their tightly packed clusters of florets as early as July but the plant will continue to flower well into the autumn. 'Gold Plate' is a popular cultivar with flat discs of golden-yellow florets up to 12cm (5½ in) across. 'Parker's Variety' is a vivid yellow, while 'Coronation Gold' is a warm mustard colour.

A.filipendulina

 9–10 ◐ · ♦♦

Acidanthera bicolor var. *murielae*

The **Peacock Lily** will, if planted in a warm sunny position, surprise you in September with a flourish of sweetly scented, orchid-shaped blooms. Closely related to the gladiolus, it should be treated in the same fashion: except in mild locations, the bulbs should be lifted as soon as the foliage has died down and stored in dry peat or sand in a cool dry shed or garage. Planting out should be done in April or May in groups of eight or ten with bulbs 10cm (4in) apart and about 6cm (2¼ in) below the surface. As cut flowers they last well in a cool room provided that the water is changed every other day.

A.bicolor var. murielae

 9–10 ○ ♦

Ailanthus altissima

A.altissima

The **Tree of Heaven** sometimes makes an immensely tall tree but in the UK seldom attains more than 20cm (66ft) and that only after very many years. It does, however, grow rapidly in its early stages, quickly becoming an attractive specimen tree with elegant foliage drooping in long fronds casting a dappled shade. Within twenty years it could be 12m (40ft) tall. The ailanthus tree is usually either male or female and the female is the better garden plant because in autumn it is hung with thousands of bunches of winged keys, similar to those of the ash, which turn a rich, dark red colour when ripe and finally whirl away helicopter-fashion on the November gales.

Amaryllis belladonna

A.belladonna

The **Belladonna Lily** is an outstandingly attractive late-flowering bulb from southern Africa. Its lovely display of pale pink trumpet-shaped flowers in September often lasts for several weeks unless hit by frost. It thrives best in a warm, well-drained spot at the foot of a south-facing wall where it can bake in the summer sunshine. The foliage appears shortly before the flowers, stands through the winter (becoming steadily more dog-eared), and dies down in early summer; on no account should it be removed before it has dried off completely. In cold districts, plant the bulbs in mid-summer about 12cm (5½ in) deep; in mild areas half that depth will suffice.

 9–10

AUTUMN

Anemone × hybrida

'Prinz Heinrich'

'Honorine Jobert'

The tall border anemones are commonly known as **Japanese Anemones** but include species other than *A. japonica*. Most people go by the cultivar name anyway and ignore the finer points of botanical distinction. Usually growing up to 150cm (5ft) tall, they will tolerate almost any conditions except deep shade and once established will form substantial clumps. 'September Charm' gives crowds of warm, pink single flowers on long stems when many other herbaceous plants are over, and white cultivars such as 'White Queen' and 'Honorine Jobert' are equally attractive. There are also semi-double cultivars such as 'Bressingham Glow' but these are not so widely available.

 9–11

Aster amellus

'King George'

These attractive border plants are closely related to the Michaelmas daisies (*Aster novi-belgii*) but produce single flowers on long stems instead of sprays. 'King George' is one of the most attractive cultivars with masses of deep, violet-blue flowers, while other cultivars are also very popular for the border. They thrive in a sunny position on well-drained soil. An established clump in flower will stand about 60cm (24in) tall and 40cm (16in) across. New plants can be obtained by dividing the clumps in spring but they should not be disturbed in autumn.

 9–11

AUTUMN

Aster novae-belgii

'Winston S. Churchill'

'Audrey'

Michaelmas Daisies are available in an impressive range of colours and heights from the rich, ruby-red flowers of 'Winston S. Churchill', usually about 80cm (33in) tall, to the compact, mauve-blue mounds of 'Audrey' which, at only 30cm (12in) tall, make a welcome splash of colour at the front of a border. They require a sunny position on well-drained soil and will rapidly form a clump up to 40cm (16in) across. Care should be taken to dead-head the plants as soon as they have flowered to prevent them from setting seed — otherwise you could soon find your original plants swamped by straggly, mongrel seedlings which bear little resemblance to their glorious pedigree parents.

 9-10 ○

Callicarpa bodinieri

C.bodinieri

This is a shrub that loves the company of its own kind and the best autumn display is obtained by planting a close group of two or three in a sunny spot. They seldom do well in exposed situations or where there is the likelihood of prolonged, hard frost. In autumn the foliage turns a warm, dark rose colour contrasting attractively with the clusters of lilac-coloured berries. **Callicarpas** have a neat, compact shape and eventually attain a height of about 3m (10ft). If necessary they can be carefully pruned in late winter. The most popular form is *C.bodinieri* 'Giraldii' because of its neat habit and reliable berrying. 'Profusion' also gives a good autumn display.

○ ◆◆

AUTUMN

Chrysanthemum

'Janet Wells'

'Margaret'

C.rubellum 'Duchess of Edinburgh'

Autumn-flowering
Chrysanthemums provide bold
splashes of colour in the border
and require minimal attention.
Their slightly bitter, spicy smell
is one of the most distinctive
scents of autumn. The display
begins with the Early Flowering
Spray types such as 'Autumn
Melody' and 'Pamela' and
Chrysanthemum rubellum
cultivars like 'Duchess of
Edinburgh' and 'Clara Curtis'.
Both types are usually between
80cm (2¾ ft) and 120cm (4ft)
tall. A variation in flower shape
comes slightly later with the
Garden Pompon types. The
brilliant orange and crimson
'Bright Eyes' and the rosy-red
favourite 'Anastasia' are just two
of the many available and their
vigorous, bushy little plants are
usually between 50cm and
70cm (20–28in) tall

 9-12

Cimicifuga cordifolia

C.cordifolia

This most attractive herbaceous
plant enjoys a moist position in
light shade. The tall plumes of
white flowers stand well clear of
the bushy mound of dark green
foliage, often attaining a height
of 120cm (4ft). In a border it
makes a pleasing contrast to
Anemone × hybrida (see page
173) and enjoys much the same
sort of treatment although it
does perhaps require more
moisture. Once established it
will form large clumps which, if
they become too big, can be
divided in the spring and a
portion replanted while the rest
are given away. Care should be
taken that the new plants are
kept well watered until they are
established.

 9–10

AUTUMN

Clematis flammula and *Clematis tangutica*

C. flammula

C. tangutica

These vigorous climbers will ramble happily through trelliswork or the branches of a tree. From late summer until well into October *Clematis flammula* (the **Fragrant Virgin's Bower**) bears small, greenish-white flowers which give off one of the sweetest perfumes ever found in a garden. The graceful sea-green foliage of *Clematis tangutica* forms a handsome background to the early autumn display of orange-yellow, lantern-shaped flowers which are gradually succeeded by balls of silky seedheads which hang like silver Christmas baubles until they are dispersed by the wind. Both plants can be pruned back hard in early spring if necessary but are better left alone except for the removal of dead wood.

🌹 9–10 ◐ ●●●

Clerodendrum trichotomum

This interesting Chinese shrub was introduced into the UK in the late nineteenth century and is commonly called the **Glory Tree**. It is an excellent plant for autumn effect when planted in a well-drained position in full sun. Carefully trained, it can even be grown as a small tree ultimately reaching 4m or 5m (13–16ft) tall. The white, star-shaped, sweetly scented flowers appear in late summer followed by a profusion of turquoise-blue berries, each set in a rich, maroon calyx. The form 'Fargesii' is particularly popular because of its smoother foliage and readiness to fruit more freely.

'Fargesii'

🌹 9 ○ ●●

AUTUMN

Colchicum autumnale and *Colchicum speciosum*

C.autumnale

C.speciosum 'The Giant'

Commonly known as **Naked Boys** or **Naked Ladies**, colchicums are also (incorrectly) referred to as autumn crocus. *Colchicum autumnale* will live contentedly in sun or semi-shade at the edge of a shrubbery or naturalized in a lawn. Apart from the usual pinky-lilac form there are white and double forms but these latter are seldom offered commercially. *Colchicum speciosum* flowers later but is better adapted to life as a garden plant. Bulbs planted in late summer in sun or semi-shade will multiply themselves into substantial clumps if left undisturbed for a few seasons. Cultivars include the huge white 'Album', the beautiful, lilac double 'Water Lily' and the deep lilac-mauve 'The Giant'.

 9

Cornus alba 'Sibirica'

'Sibirica'

The **Westonbirt Dogwood** is an attractive deciduous shrub rarely exceeding 2m (6½ ft) in height, with good autumnal foliage. Most gardeners, however, grow it for the lovely bright scarlet stems that suddenly catch the eye as the leaves fall. The best colour is in the young stems so the whole shrub is usually pruned back to the base every March. The stems offer a vivid contrast when planted in association with evergreens and, while not being especially fussy as to position, the plant should obviously be placed where the winter sunshine will spotlight it.

177

Cotoneaster dammeri and *Cotoneaster horizontalis*

C.dammeri

C.horizontalis

Cotoneaster dammeri is a completely prostrate evergreen which hugs the ground. The long trailing sprays of white flowers in mid-summer are followed by a profusion of bright red berries contrasting vividly with the rich, dark foliage. *Cotoneaster horizontalis* is a marvellous plant for a low north-facing wall or sloping bank. Its autumnal fruits are briefly surpassed by a glorious display of red and gold autumn foliage which then drops, leaving the fan-shaped branches studded with a beautiful pattern of bright red berries. Other species of cotoneaster provide graceful berry-bearing shrubs such as *C.conspicuus* or small trees like *C.* × 'Cornubia'.

 6–7

Crinum × powellii

C. × powellii

The **Cape Coast Lily** flourishes best in a sunny border or, in cooler regions, against a south-facing wall. The flower stems begin to emerge in August and, if the season has been dry, the plant should be copiously watered each evening to ensure that it succeeds in delivering the lovely display of pendulous pink or white lily-shaped flowers. The bulbs are enormous and when planting (usually in late spring) the shoulders should be between 15cm and 25cm (6–10in) below the surface. A winter covering of ashes or bracken litter would be a wise precaution in cold districts. Once planted they may be left undivided and undisturbed for many years.

 8–10

AUTUMN

Crocus sativus and Crocus speciosus

C.sativus

C.speciosus

Crocus sativus needs a sunny position where the bulbs can ripen well and it should be fed with liquid fertilizer as soon as the flowers are over. It is called the **Saffron Crocus** because saffron is obtained by drying and crushing the orange-red stigmas from the centre of the flower. *Crocus speciosus* is the true **Autumn Crocus**; its pale mauve flowers appear in October and, once established in a border or rough grass, will spread itself by seed and by producing cormlets. Corms should be planted at least 5cm (2in) deep and *C.speciosus* will tolerate fairly poor soil provided it gets good light for most of the winter and spring.

 9–10 ◑ ♦♦

Cyclamen hederifolium

C.hederifolium

Frequently sold under its old name *C.neapolitanum*, its delightful pink or white flowers and endless variety of leaf shapes and markings make an attractive patch at the path's edge or the base of a tree. Newly purchased tubers must be planted the right way up. Roots are produced only on the upper surface together with short knobbly protrusions which grow into flowers and leaves. The tuber is usually slightly saucer-shaped with a hollow on the upper side and should be planted about 5cm (2½ in) deep in semi-shade. The white *C.hederifolium* 'Album' is harder to obtain and often twice the price of the pink form.

 9–12 ◑ ♦♦

AUTUMN

Dahlias

'House of Orange'

'Comet'

'J.S. Bach'

'Little William'

Without these vividly coloured flowers that grow in such a variety of shapes and sizes, the herbaceous border would be very dull indeed after the end of August. In mild areas you can dodge the chore of lifting the tubers after the first frost, storing them in dry peat and replanting them again the following May, but in cold districts you will probably lose them if you leave them in the ground over the winter. As with chrysanthemums, there are a great many cultivars bred purely for the show bench and while their huge shaggy heads and blinding colours win all sorts of cups and medals they do look dreadfully out of place in the average garden.

For the border, types such as the Anemone Flowered cultivars like 'Bambino' are popular, growing about 40cm (16in) high and offering plenty of flowers for cutting as well as garden decoration. The taller-growing Decorative types come in all colours from the almost black 'Arabian Night' to pure white 'Snow Bunting' and with brilliant colours such as 'House of Orange' too. These usually stand up to 90cm (3ft) tall. Pompons are also prized for their tight, neatly-shaped flowers, and plants like the delightful purple and white 'Little William' are very popular. Finally, the Cactus Flowered cultivars standing about 130cm (4¼ ft) tall lend an exotic touch. Cultivars such as the pure yellow 'J.S. Bach' or deep, orange-red 'Clarion' look especially cheerful on grey early autumn days.

🌹 8–10 ○ ◗◗

Erica carnea and Erica vagans

E.carnea 'Foxhollow'

E.vagans 'Lyonesse'

Erica carnea is a popular **Heather**, widely grown for its attractive, weed-smothering foliage. Being lime-tolerant it can be used in situations where other heathers will not thrive. The golden foliage of 'Foxhollow' or 'Westwood Yellow', the bronze 'Vivelli' or bright green 'Springwood White' associate well with dwarf conifers. Erica vagans is only slightly lime-tolerant but generally flowers earlier than E.carnea. The white flowered 'Lyonesse' or cerise 'Mrs D.F.Maxwell' are especially good for carrying colour interest into the autumn. Both species grow between 30cm and 45cm (12-18in) tall and demand an open sunny position.

 9–11 ○ ◆◆

Ginkgo biloba

G.biloba

The **Maidenhair Tree** is grown largely for its curiosity value but it does provide a glorious autumn display of clear golden-yellow foliage before finally dropping its fan-shaped leaves. Tolerant of most soil types including chalk and thriving even in areas of severe atmospheric pollution, it will attain a height of 8m (26ft) in twenty years but could ultimately grow as high as 25m (82ft) in its magnificent old age. Long considered extinct, it is now known, by comparing present-day plants with fossil records, to have survived virtually unchanged for over 150 million years.

○

AUTUMN

Hippophae rhamnoides

H.rhamnoides (f.)

The **Sea Buckthorn** can be used as a tall (3m/10ft) windbreak hedge in coastal areas or grown as a small group in any garden. The female plants bear brilliant orange-yellow berries normally shunned by birds and so giving an attractive appearance throughout the late autumn and winter. To ensure a crop, a male plant must be nearby. The elegant, silvery willow-like foliage offers a cool contrast to the many vivid colours of high summer, and planted at the end of a view it will lend an illusion of distance. Sharp spines on its branches are another good reason for using it as a hedge where animals are a nuisance.

Liquidambar styraciflua

L.styraciflua

The **Sweet Gum** is another of those trees with brilliant crimson autumn foliage and is often confused with the maples because of its similar leaf shape. Tolerant of all except shallow chalky soils, it is sometimes at risk in the first two or three seasons from frost but is perfectly hardy once established. It will reach a height of 6m (20ft) within twenty years but could eventually achieve as much as 45m (150ft) when mature. Because of its narrow upright shape it is quite suitable for even relatively small gardens. The clone 'Lane Roberts' is popular for its reliable autumn colour and smoother bark, while 'Variegata' has handsome, creamy margined leaves which gradually flush rose-pink in late summer.

AUTUMN

Liriodendron tulipifera

'Aureomarginata'

The **Tulip Tree** always attracts interest in a garden, particularly on a sunny October day when the clear butter-yellow autumnal foliage glows so brilliantly. The large leaves are most unusually shaped. Being fast growing and succeeding in any reasonably fertile soil it makes a good specimen tree in a lawn or at the edge of a small garden. Liriodendron flowers are most attractive but rarely seen because they do not begin to appear until the tree is well established and then often only near the top. Within twenty years the tree could be as much as 12m (40ft) tall and will ultimately attain about 50m (164ft). The variegated form, 'Aureomarginata', is more suitable for a smallish garden.

🌸 6 ○ 💧💧

Liriope muscari and *Liriope spicata alba*

L.muscari

The flat rush-like foliage of *Liriope muscari* provides good ground cover for areas in sun or light shade. Four or five plants grouped about 40cm (16in) apart will soon form a dense, weed-resistant clump. It dislikes lime but spreads rapidly on acid soil and gives a delightful display of mauve flower spikes, about 30cm (12in) high, in September and October. The white species *Liriope spicata alba* is fully evergreen and produces its spikes of flowers somewhat later than its cousin. It is also a little more difficult to obtain but well worth planting if it can be found.

🌸 9–10 ◐ 💧💧💧

AUTUMN

Malus 'John Downie'

'John Downie'

This charming **Crab Apple** would make a delightful small tree for even the tiniest of gardens. It rarely exceeds 5m or 6m (16–19½ ft) tall and its spread can be curtailed if necessary by careful pruning as soon as the flowers have dropped. The white spring blossom is beautiful but brief, but the dazzling display of rich orange-red fruits makes the tree a feature for several weeks in autumn, unless picked to make crab apple jelly which is often their fate. The tree will thrive in any fertile garden soil and will blossom and fruit more freely if treated to a dose of general purpose fertilizer in spring before the buds burst.

 3 ○

Nerine bowdenii

N. bowdenii

Commonly known as the **Guernsey Lily** and sometimes as the **Diamond Lily**, this is yet another beautiful, pink flowered bulb from southern Africa. It is really reliably hardy only in the south and west of England or in sheltered gardens where it is protected from the worst of the winter frost. Having flowered in the first season after planting, the lilies will often then take two or three seasons to establish themselves before flowering again; thereafter they will provide a steadily increasing display of exotic, sugar-pink blooms each autumn. Plant the bulbs in a warm, sunny position with the neck of the bulb just below the surface of the soil and do not disturb once established.

 10-11 ○

AUTUMN

Nyssa sylvatica

N.sylvatica

North America has given many handsome trees to European gardens and when it comes to autumn colour the **Tupelo** may arguably be its finest contribution. It must be planted young because it hates being moved once established and it prefers a moist, lime-free soil. Although slow growing it will attain some 5m (16ft) in height within twenty years and eventually reach 30m (100ft) in maturity. Since it has a compact, upright habit it is very suitable for fairly restricted sites but its dark, glossy foliage will cast quite a deep shade. In autumn the long oval leaves gradually turn brilliant shades of scarlet, orange and yellow until the whole tree seems ablaze.

 6 ○

Ornithogalum thyrsiodes

O.thyrsiodes

The **Chincherinchee** is one of the most popular of florists' flowers because of its ability to last so long in water. The bulbs will grow happily in any sunny, well-drained corner and, if planted in April, will oblige with a display of blooms in late August or September of the same year. In very dry summers the plants should be kept well watered. Set the bulbs about 10cm (4in) deep and 7cm (2¾ in) apart in small groups. The spikes of white, star-shaped flowers normally stand about 30cm (12in) high and good blooms for the following season can be encouraged by giving the plants a liquid feed after the flowers have faded.

 7-10 ○

Parthenocissus quinquefolia and *Parthenocissus tricuspidata*

P. quinquefolia

P. tricuspidata

The common names of these two handsome, self-clinging climbers are often confused. **Virginia Creeper** is *P.quinquefolia*, while **Boston Ivy** is *P.tricuspidata*. Both will rapidly clothe a large wall but neither should be used unless there is plenty of room for them to spread. Provided that the wall up which they climb is sound in the first place they will do no damage at all, but regular inspections of guttering and drainpipes are advisable. The rich, scarlet and orange autumnal foliage of both species is a truly wonderful sight. They are quite unfussy as to situation but care should be taken to secure them if they are likely to be exposed to summer gales.

5

Pernettya mucronata

P. mucronata

These dense, wiry little South American evergreen shrubs offer a wide choice of berry colours in autumn from the unblemished 'White Pearl' to the dark purple 'Mulberry Wine'. Planted in groups of three or four in sun or light shade they will quickly form a dense thicket about 90cm (3ft) high studded, in autumn, with a dazzling display of berries that often last right through the winter. They prefer a lime-free soil and, although not strictly dioecious, will give the best display of berries if a male clone is included in the group. 'Thymifolia' is one such clone with delicate foliage and profuse white flowers in May but it is hard to obtain.

6

Polygonum macrophyllum

P. macrophyllum

Although somewhat slow growing, this late-flowering species is a very useful low plant for the front of a border. The spikes of baby-pink flowers stand about 45cm (18in) high above a mound of wavy strap-like foliage. They make a pleasing contrast to dahlias or early-flowering chrysanthemums. They will tolerate any soil type and thrive equally well in sun or light shade. However, they dislike very dry situations so a generous helping of compost or peat when planting will pay dividends. Unlike some of its very vigorous and invasive relatives this particular polygonum will not take over the entire border and choke most of your other favourites; it simply stays where it's put.

   8-11

Prunus sargentii

P. sargentii

While most **Ornamental Cherries** are grown solely for their spring blossom, this lovely species gives additional value for money. In spring the display of pink flowers is delightful but in autumn it is one of the first trees to change colour, turning a rich mixture of orange and crimson shades in late September. After twenty years it will have attained a height of about 9m (30ft) and will make a further 4 or 5m (13–16ft) after that. Its broad, round head requires plenty of space, say 3m (10ft) in each direction. It is happiest on lime or chalky soils in an open sunny position and will be an asset to any garden.

 3-4

AUTUMN

Pyracantha 'Mojave'

'Mojave'

Firethorns are very useful evergreen shrubs for growing against a north- or east-facing wall and can reach as high as 5m (16ft). If grown as a free-standing bush they are usually shorter but equally attractive. The autumn display of brilliant orange or yellow berries against the bright green foliage is most striking. The red-berried cultivar 'Mojave' and its pale orange-berried sister 'Shawnee' are resistant to fireblight and scab disease. When being trained against a wall, the long shoots should be pruned back to just above the flowering spur as soon as the blossom has faded. Newly planted specimens should be kept well watered during their first season.

Rhus typhina

R. typhina

The **Staghorn Sumach** makes a sizeable, exotic-looking shrub in light, well-drained soil and grows equally well in sun or light shade. The brilliant colours of its autumn foliage look especially striking against a screen of evergreens or a light coloured wall. Even with careful training it will seldom exceed 3m (10ft) in height but could well develop a sideways spread of 3 or 4m (10–13ft) unless controlled. Care should be taken when pruning because the sap is poisonous and causes irritation to skin or eyes. If pruned to the ground every February it makes a showy clump of exotic foliage in a sunny border; an unusual alternative to hostas or ferns.

AUTUMN

Rose 'Elmshorn' and *Rosa moyesii*

'Elmshorn'

R. moyesii

'Elmshorn' is an attractive, bright pink single rose which, if left unpruned, produces a second flush of flowers in autumn that often surpasses its summer display. It is not always easy to obtain but well worth hunting for. *Rosa moyesii* is another handsome, medium-sized shrub which gives autumn value, this time in the form of bright crimson flagon-shaped heps. Both plants should not be pruned except to remove dead wood and weak straggly shoots. This is best done in February when you can see the overall shape of the bush. *R.moyesii* will make a dome-shaped shrub of about 3m (10ft) tall while 'Elmshorn' will attain a height and spread of about 150cm (5ft).

 7-9 ○ ◆◆

Schizostylis coccinea

'Mrs Hegarty'

The **Kaffir Lily** will often flower from mid-autumn until well into the winter. It is quite hardy and thrives in light shade or a moist sunny border. The 60cm (24in) tall spikes of pink or scarlet flowers are beautiful for cutting at a time when there is very little else suitable in the garden. 'Viscountess Byng' and 'Mrs Hegarty' are a lovely pale pink and flower later than the deep scarlet cultivar 'Major'. A mixed planting gives a patch of colour lasting about three months. The rhizomes should be set just below the surface of the soil and should be lifted and divided in springtime every three years to ensure continued flowering.

 9-11 ○ ◆◆

AUTUMN

Sedum spectabile

'Autumn Joy'

The **Ice Plant** is useful for a hot dry spot and its wide flat heads of pink flowers in early autumn are most attractive. The glaucous blue-grey foliage makes a good foil for summer-flowering border plants and the flat, dark brown seedheads look very handsome in the winter until they are pruned off to make way for the new growth. 'Autumn Joy' is deservedly popular for its large salmon-pink flowerheads standing some 60cm (24in) high in tight, well-disciplined clumps, while 'Variegatum' is prized for its interesting buff-yellow marked foliage as well as its dark pink flowers. Over-large clumps can be divided in early spring.

 8-10

Sorbus aucuparia 'Xanthocarpa' and *Sorbus* 'Joseph Rock'

S. aucuparia 'Xanthocarpa'

Sorbus 'Joseph Rock'

Sorbus aucuparia is familiar to most people as **Mountain Ash**. Tolerant of any soil and unfussy as to position, it will reach a height of 8m (26ft) within twenty years. The cultivar 'Xanthocarpa' has amber-yellow berries instead of the bright orange common to this species, and it seems less prone to being stripped by birds. 'Joseph Rock' is a hybrid of unknown origin and has been an outstandingly popular garden tree for many years enjoying the same conditions and treatment as *S.aucuparia*. The brilliant orange, copper and purple autumn foliage forms a superb setting for the large clusters of creamy-yellow berries which become deep amber when mature and hold long after the foliage has fallen.

 6

AUTUMN

Sternbergia lutea

S. lutea

This attractive, crocus-shaped flower from the eastern Mediterranean is said by some to be the 'Lily of the Field' referred to in the Bible. It thrives in a warm sunny position at the front of a border and is particularly at home on chalky soils. The large, bright yellow flowers emerge at the same time as the foliage, usually in late September or early October, but being only 12cm (5½ in) tall must be planted where they can be easily seen. The form *S. lutea* 'Augustifolia' is freer flowering but not easy to find.

The bulbs are comparatively large and should be set about 5cm (2in) below the surface.

 9-10 ○

Symphoricarpus albus

S. albus

The **Snowberry** is another North American native which has found favour in Europe. Although it will grow well in the shade of trees or buildings, the best displays of berries are obtained from plants growing in sun or light shade. While it never attains much more than 150cm (5ft) in height it produces suckers freely from its roots and gradually forms a dense thicket several metres across unless carefully pruned in March of each year. The abundant display of poisonous white berries is left untouched by birds and normally lasts well into the winter long after the foliage has dropped, but do not plant where small children might be tempted to taste the fruit.

 7 ●

FERNS, BAMBOOS and GRASSES

While, for most gardeners, colour is an essential ingredient in garden design, there remains a specific need for plants whose striking shapes and beautiful foliage provide a distinctive contrast or a cool background to flowering plants. Ferns, of course, never flower, and with bamboos and grasses the flowers are usually green or buff and are so much an integral part of the plant that they are rarely thought of as flowers at all — except in the case of the graceful plumes of pampas grass (*Cortaderia*).

FERNS, BAMBOOS and GRASSES

Asplenium scolopendrium cristatum

Athyrium filix-femina

Osmunda regalis

Polystichum setiferum

FERNS

Four genera of fern commonly offered are *Asplenium, Athyrium, Osmunda* and *Polystichum* although there are many more obtainable from specialist nurseries.

Asplenium scolopendrium is commonly known as the **Hart's Tongue Fern** and forms an attractive mound of rich green foliage about 45cm (18in) high and 30cm (12in) across. An interesting variant is the form known as *A.scolopendrium cristatum* which has a fascinating crest or tassel on the upper part of the leaf. They like a rich moist soil in semi-shade and thrive particularly well on chalk or limestone soils.

Athyrium filix-femina is a British woodland native usually known as the **Lady Fern**. Its graceful lacy foliage is particularly useful for giving a slightly wild effect in a semi-shaded spot beneath trees or among rhododendrons. It makes an attractive arching shape about 80cm (2¾ft) tall and 40cm (16in) across although the form *A.filix-femina vernoniae* (if you can obtain it) can be as much as 110cm (3½ft) tall and 80cm (2¾ft) across if you require a more substantial plant. It grows well in light shade but requires plenty of moisture and a deep, rich, fairly neutral or slightly acid soil.

Osmunda regalis is nicknamed the **Royal Fern** and can, in ideal conditions, assume truly regal proportions. It dislikes chalk and limestone soils and requires copious amounts of moisture, so its favourite position is in light shade in a rich, peaty soil on the edge of a pond or

FERNS, BAMBOOS and GRASSES

Arundinaria nitida

Arundinaria viridistriata

Cortaderia selloana

stream. It will grow up to 130cm (4¼ ft) tall each year and in time could form a broad clump anything up to 2m (6½ ft) across — but such a spread will take many years. The fronds turn a rich reddish-brown in winter and, if harvested, make a good winter mulch for dahlias, acidantheras, zantedeschias and other plants which need a little extra shelter from frost.

The two most frequently offered species of *Polystichum* are *Polystichum polyblepharum* and *Polystichum setiferum* and both are excellent garden plants. They are at their best in moist, well-drained soil in partial shade. *P.polyblepharum* is equally striking in summer and winter: it has brilliant green foliage during the summer months which dies but remains fully erect for the whole of the winter until it is displaced by new foliage the following spring. It rarely grows more than 50cm (20in) tall with a spread of 40cm (16in). The **Soft Shield Fern**, *P.setiferum*, is another native of British woodlands and adapts readily to garden use. The elegant spear-shaped fronds uncurl themselves gracefully in an intriguing fashion from mid-May onwards, forming a bold clump up to 100cm (3¼ ft) tall and 60cm (2ft) across — although the form *P.setiferum divisilobum* will seldom attain even half that size.

BAMBOOS

Bamboos are becoming popular but, except at specialist nurseries, it is unlikely that you will be offered any genus other than *Arundinaria*, and in most cases only three or four species of that. Apart from being very thirsty plants which therefore require a very moist site, bamboos are quite unfussy as to soil type. Except for some of the rarer species, they are evergreen and perfectly hardy, preferring a site in good light but sheltered from strong north or east winds. They make good screens around a garage or shed or on the south- or west-facing side of a wall or hedge.

A useful species, if you have room for it, is *Arundinaria anceps*. It grows up to 3m (10ft) tall and a thirty-year-old clump can be anything up to 4m (13ft) across, although it is possible to keep the plant in check by harvesting and drying the canes for use in the garden.

The other two species of *Arundinaria* most commonly offered are *Arundinaria murieliae* and *Arundinaria nitida* which are quite similar to one another in size and habit. Both make graceful spreading clumps up to 3m (10ft) high and in ten years the clump will be about 1m (3¼ft) across at the base. Because of the arching sweep of the canes, the spread at its widest point could be anything up to 3m (10ft) across, casting a dappled and constantly changing shade as the stems move in the slightest breeze.

It is often possible to find *Arundinaria viridistriata*. This beautifully variegated green and gold bamboo with its chocolate-coloured canes rarely grows more than 120cm (4ft) tall, but it is sometimes rather invasive and in just five years a clump can attain a spread of 150cm (5ft). It will continue to expand unless you dig it up, divide it and replant only a portion of it every five or six years. Again, it requires plenty of moisture and an open position sheltered from north or east winds.

The temptation to cut bamboo and use it for background foliage in flower arrangements should be resisted since the leaves curl up and die after only a couple of hours in water. There is really no easy way to keep it fresh.

GRASSES

The ornamental grasses commercially offered range from the enormously tall pampas grass (*Cortaderia*), through the tall and medium height *Miscanthus* to the ground-hugging *Carex* and *Festuca* species so useful for dry, shaded banks or as ground cover among low-growing perennials.

Cortaderia selloana, the ever popular **Pampas Grass,** is available in several forms and makes a striking specimen growing alone in the centre of a lawn or paved area or as part of a border scheme. The foliage of *C.selloana* itself will stand about 150cm (5ft) high and form a clump up to 100cm (3¼ft) across, while the plumes of flowers will stand as high as 3m (10ft). For the smaller garden there is a more compact form, *C.selloana* 'Pumila', which makes a clump about 80cm (2¾ft) tall and 60cm (24in) across with plumes up to 2m (6½ft) tall; there is also an even more compact cultivar, 'Silver Comet', becoming more widely available which attains a height

Miscanthus sinensis 'Zebrinus'

Festuca glauca

Carex morrowii 'Evergold'

Phalaris arundinacea 'Picta'

of only 60cm (24in) and a spread of 40cm (16in) with plumes standing only 120cm (4ft) tall. The variegated cultivar of *C.selloana*, 'Gold Band', is of similar size and habit to 'Pumila' but has broad, gold bands down the leaf. All pampas grasses can be kept within acceptable bounds by lifting and dividing in April every four or five years. In areas likely to suffer severe frost they should be protected with a straw or bracken mulch for the first winter after planting or replanting. The trick of burning out the old leaves from the centre of the clump by soaking it in parafin and dropping in a lighted match is very dangerous and likely to kill the plant unless you know exactly what you are doing. Even a moderate breeze will send flames shooting out a metre or more on all sides and you could well find that more than just the plant gets scorched.

Most of the *Miscanthus* offered are forms of *Miscanthus sinensis* and grow anything between 150cm and 230cm (5 − 7½ ft) tall according to cultivar. *Miscanthus sinensis purpureus* is an upright-growing plant forming a dense clump 150cm (5ft) tall with a spread of about 100cm (3¼ ft) after five years; its foliage has an attractive purplish tinge. The cultivar 'Zebrinus' grows to about 2m (6½ ft) tall and will make a spreading clump of 100cm (3¼ ft) across within five years, while 'Silver Feather' is even taller at 220cm (7ft) and spreading up to 120cm (4ft). Another species of *Miscanthus* is *Miscanthus sacchariflorus* which is an excellent plant for a screen or windbreak. In its first year after planting it will attain a height of about 150cm to 200cm (5 – 6½ft), but once established it will grow up to 2.5m or 3m (8 – 10ft) tall each year, dying back to the base in winter. The previous year's foliage can be cut down in February or March as the new growth begins, and a row of plants 45cm (18in) apart will soon form an elegant and unusual screen. Being non-invasive it will not get out of hand and start to strangle other plants close to it. If you require a really dense screen then you should plant a staggered double row with the plants 60cm (24in) apart and the rows also 60cm apart.

Festuca glauca and *Festuca scoparia* are two attractive, small, hummock-forming species which make good ground cover and succeed quite happily even in dry shade. Both are evergreen and require the minimum of attention. *F.glauca* has strikingly handsome blue-grey foliage standing up to 25cm (10in) high and forming a mound 30cm (12in) across, while *F.scoparia* is a brilliant emerald green, stands only 15cm (6in) tall and forms a cushion up to 20cm (8in) across. The *Carex* usually offered is *Carex morrowii,* and the cultivar 'Evergold' is particularly attractive. The long golden leaves with their bright green margins form a bold mound about 20cm (8in) tall and 40cm (16in) across and it makes a very worthwhile ground-cover plant or an attractive contrast plant at the front of a border. It also looks very handsome in a paved area if one slab is left out and

planted with the grass to relieve the plainness of a large area of stone.

You may also come across *Phalaris arundinacea* 'Picta', an attractive silvery-green variegated grass which grows to about 60cm (24in) tall and makes a clump up to 40cm (16in) across within three years. It is often snapped up simply because of its charming nickname, **Gardeners' Garters**, but it may prove too invasive for a small garden. If you do buy it, allow it plenty of room to spread or else lift and divide the clump every three or four years.

TUBS, TROUGHS, WINDOW BOXES AND HANGING-BASKETS

(A table showing the size and requirements of the plants mentioned is given on pages 206-7 at the end of this section.)

Planted containers add an extra dimension to gardens, particularly those which are very small and enclosed by high boundary walls or fences. Indeed, if all you have is a flat roof, tiny patio or balcony, then this type of gardening is virtually your only option, but it is by no means a restricted one, nor is it a difficult way in which to grow plants.

TUBS and BOXES

Begonia semperflorens

Hedera helix sagittaefolia 'Variegata'

Calceolaria herbeohybrida

Impatiens 'Elfin Red'

As far as the question of 'which comes first, the container or the plant?' is concerned, it really is simplest if you settle on the container first and then see how you can fill it with plants.

For a narrow passageway at the side of a house, a trellis attached to the wall can support several semi-circular baskets at various levels. The addition of a couple of troughs resting on the ground at the foot of the wall can completely transform a dull area and help to bring the garden right round to the back door.

Tender perennials and shrubs, such as pelargoniums, *Felicias*, fuchsias and oleanders grown in pots and protected indoors during the winter, can be arranged in attractively haphazard groups interspersed with hardy evergreen shrubs such as *Aucubas*, dwarf conifers, camellias and sweet bay (*Laurus nobilis*) to give a patio or a paved area beside a pool a Mediterranean look.

The area outside a basement flat can become a garden below normal ground level with a couple of clematis in large pots reaching up towards the sunshine at street level and underplanted with ferns or ivies; and the careful positioning of a large mirror or two can deceive the eye into believing that the space is far larger than it really is.

The façade of an older-style, multi-occupied building, such as a Victorian block of flats or a house which has been split into several apartments, can be immeasurably brightened up by window boxes. Some

TUBS and BOXES

Iberis umbellata and *Pelargonium peltatum* 'Roulette'

Lavatera 'Silver Cup'

Ageratum 'Blue Mink'

Lobelia 'Blue Basket'

modern developments such as the Barbican in London actually encourage residents to put window boxes and troughs on to their balconies. The random nature of the planting, reflecting the different tastes and preferences of the residents responsible for them, creates fascinating and constantly changing patterns and gives as much pleasure to those who are simply passing by as to the actual owners of the apartments.

With any form of container gardening, the most important point to watch is watering. All containers should have a generous layer of small stones or broken flowerpot shards in the bottom and adequate drainage holes so that surplus water can drain away. If the drainage is poor, then the roots of the plants will become waterlogged and eventually suffocate and rot. The compost filling the container should usually be a peat-based one so that moisture retention is good. This combination of a moist soil and good drainage provides ideal growing conditions, but it must be remembered that the plants will take up water pretty rapidly in spring and summer — especially where they are exposed to drying winds or long hours of sunshine — so the containers must be checked daily to see if they need watering. Water until it runs out of the bottom drainage holes to give a thorough soaking. Where possible, always water in the evening so that the moisture is available to the plants in the very early morning, which is the time

TUBS and BOXES

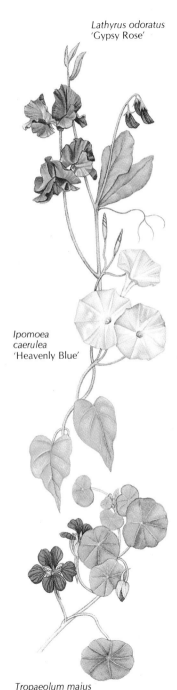

Lathyrus odoratus 'Gypsy Rose'

Ipomoea caerulea 'Heavenly Blue'

Tropaeolum majus

when they take up most of their daily requirement. Don't imagine that just because the containers are outside, ordinary rainfall will be sufficient. In most cases the leaves of the plants shelter the soil in the container and, except during a monumental downpour, very little rain actually gets in. This is especially true of window boxes and hanging-baskets where they are sheltered by the building anyway.

Growing in containers can also give some people the opportunity to grow hardy plants which will not usually succeed in their garden. This is particularly the case with anybody who has chalky or alkaline soil but would like to grow camellias and rhododendrons. In large tubs, filled with a lime-free compost, these lovely shrubs grow very well and eventually attain an impressive stature. They need to be fed regularly, of course, and it is sometimes advisable to change the soil in the container every five or six years. If you live in an area where the tap water is 'hard', i.e. containing a lot of dissolved lime, then you must not irrigate lime-hating plants with it; instead, you must provide a source of rainwater from a butt or else boil the water first and allow it to cool so that the lime is boiled out.

By the same token, people whose garden soil is acid, but who are particularly drawn to those lime-loving rock garden plants such as rockery *Dianthus*, dwarf tulips, *Aubrieta* and *Gypsophila*, may find that the most satisfactory way of indulging their special interest

TUBS and BOXES

Dianthus deltoides

Tulipa tarda

Tulipa pulchella humilis

is by using stone troughs filled with lime-enriched compost and planted as miniature rockeries.

Trough gardens, raised to about waist height, can also provide an interest for disabled members of a household or for those who have grown too old to be able to cope with the constant kneeling or bending required in the routine cultivation of a garden. Gardening of this kind often allows for the continuation of a much loved hobby or alternatively provides a new interest to replace or supplement other hobbies.

Having settled the question of which container you are going to use and where it is to be sited, you must then select those plants best suited to it. For a sunny, open aspect containers can be planted with many of the hardy and half-hardy annuals and tender perennials and shrubs which are found in profusion in garden centres and shops during April and May. A large tub planted with hollyhocks (*Althaea rosea*), *Lavatera* 'Silver Cup' or 'Mont Blanc', *Molucella* (Bells of Ireland) or other similar upright growing annuals, and underplanted with trailing *Lobelia*, the compact, bushy *Ageratum* 'Blue Mink' or forget-me-not (*Myosotis*), will make a striking feature for most of the summer. Window boxes with *Nemesia*, pelargoniums, nasturtiums or *Celosia* guarantee colour on a sunny window sill from May to the first autumn frost. Hanging-baskets planted with love-lies-bleeding (*Amaranthus*

TUBS and BOXES

Nerium oleander

Fuchsia 'Citation'

Pelargonium zonale 'Orbit'

caudatus), candytuft (*Iberis umbellata*), *Tagetes* such as 'Tiger Eyes' or 'Naughty Marietta', fuchsias and ivy-leafed pelargoniums provide eye-level interest in a strategic position sheltered from the wind.

These annuals and tender perennials can either be planted on their own or, if you prefer, one or two dwarf or slow-growing shrubs or conifers can be permanently planted in the containers and then the bedding plants arranged around them. In large tubs the sweet bay (*Laurus nobilis*), or one of the many upright dwarf conifers, can provide a central feature; alternatively, a tripod of tall bamboo canes supporting a large flowered clematis, morning glory (*Ipomoea caerulea*) or sweet peas can serve the same function. In troughs or window boxes, trailing plants such as nasturtium or *Lobelia* can form an attractive frontage largely hiding the container, while the dwarf hardy fuchsia *F. magellanica* 'Pumila', dwarf lavenders or *Santolina* are useful small shrubs for permanent planting if required. *Coleus* makes attractive foliage plants in dazzling shades of green, gold, red and purple but many cultivars need to be regularly pinched out at the growing tip to keep them bushy and prevent them from flowering.

In shaded or semi-shaded situations your choice is more limited. *Nicotiana* always performs well, but some cultivars are too tall for use in all but the largest containers; for window boxes and smaller

TUBS and BOXES

Clematis montana 'Rubens'

Clematis alpina 'Francis Rivis'

Hedera helix 'Cuspidata Major'

tubs try to obtain one of the dwarf types such as the Tinkerbell strain which grows only about 25cm (10in) tall instead of the usual 90cm (3ft). Their colours are invariably a mixture so you can't plan a specific colour scheme. Busy Lizzy (*Impatiens*), *Begonia semperflorens, Calceolarias* and pansies all make attractive bushy plants with bright colourful flowers. Very often these are sold with some flowers already open, so here it is possible to choose the colours you prefer. *Tolmiea menziesii* is a very useful foliage plant for shady places, but it will eventually take over the entire container unless it is lifted and divided in the spring. Ivies and periwinkles (*Vinca minor*) are good trailing subjects, while trailing *Lobelia* seems equally happy in sun and shade.

More and more people are making use of window boxes to grow fresh herbs for the kitchen. In some cases it is wise to grow herbs in a 15cm (6in) flowerpot plunged up to its neck in soil in the box, otherwise they will spread aggressively and quickly take over the entire container. This is especially true of mint, chives and marjoram. The shrubby herbs such as thyme, sage and rosemary will all need to be kept carefully trimmed or else tipped out every third year and started again from cuttings, but it is often the case that an average cook will cut so much material from them in the course of the year that excessive growth does not become a problem. Parsley seldom seems to come up

TUBS and BOXES

Mentha spicata (Spearmint)

Allium schoenoprasum (Chives)

Origanum vulgare (Marjoram)

where you sow it, or else it comes up like a weed all over the box, so you may find with that particular herb that it is better to sow some seed in a pot and then transplant the seedlings into the box or else buy a pot or two from your local garden centre each year.

It is also possible to grow lettuce and tomatoes in window boxes or in a growing bag on a convenient level surface. For lettuce you are best advised to select one of the non-hearting cultivars such as 'Salad Bowl' where you simply pick off the number of leaves that you require and allow the plant to carry on growing instead of cutting the whole plant at once. These are particularly suitable for small one- or two-person households and make for far less waste. With tomatoes go for the small-fruited types such as 'Minibel' or 'Gardener's Delight' which will happily trail over the front if grown in a window box and will give a substantial crop. It is unlikely that you will be able to buy young plants of these kinds of vegetables from a garden centre or shop, but they are easily grown from seed which is widely available. A useful crop of dwarf french beans, alpine strawberries, radishes and the ball carrot 'Rondo' can also be cultivated in the same way, but in all cases it is vital to ensure that the container is never short of water.

TUBS and BOXES

Tender Shrubs, Hardy and Half-hardy Annuals and Biennials Suitable for Container Planting

KEY

H.A.	= Hardy annual		H.H.A.	= Half-hardy annual
H.B.	= Hardy biennial		T.S.	= Tender shrub
H.P.	= Hardy perennial			

Name	Height x spread	Sun/shade requirement	Type
Abutilon	90cm x 30cm (3ft x 12in)	○	T.S.
Ageratum	15cm x 15cm (6in x 6in)	◑	H.H.A.
Althaea rosea **Hollyhock**	180cm x 40cm (6ft x 16in)	◑	H.A.
Alyssum	10cm x 15cm (4in x 6in)	◑	H.A.
Amaranthus caudatus **Love-lies-bleeding**	75cm x 40cm (30in x 16in)	○	H.H.A.
Antirrhinum **Snapdragon**	up to 50cm x 30cm (up to 20in x 12in)	◑	H.A.

Aster
  dwarf compact cultivars
  chrysanthemum flowered
	20cm x 20cm
	(8in x 8in)
	up to 60cm x 30cm
	(up to 24in x 12in)
		○
		
		○
			H.H.A.
			
			H.H.A.

Begonia semperflorens	15cm x 15cm (6in x 6in)	●	H.H.A.
Calceolaria	30cm x 30cm (12in x 12in)	◑	H.H.A.
Calendula **Marigold**	40cm x 25cm (16in x 10in)	◑	H.A.
Celosia cristata	20cm x 15cm (8in x 6in)	◑	H.H.A.
Celosia plumosa **Prince of Wales' Feathers**	30cm x 20cm (12in x 8in)	◑	H.H.A.
Centaurea cyanus **Cornflower**	45cm x 20cm (18in x 8in)	○	H.A.
Cheiranthus **Wallflower**	45cm x 30cm (18in x 12in)	●	H.B.

Coleus
  dwarf
  monarch
	20cm x 15cm
	(8in x 6in)
	45cm x 30cm
	(18in x 12in)
		○
		
		○
			H.H.A.
			
			H.H.A.

Delphinium
Larkspur
  dwarf
  stock flowered
	
	30cm x 10cm
	(12in x 4in)
	90cm x 30cm
	(3ft x 12in)
		
		◑
		
		◑
			
			H.A.
			
			H.A.

Dianthus barbatus **Sweet William**	45cm x 10cm (18in x 4in)	◑	H.B.
Helichrysum **Strawflower**	30cm x 10cm (12in x 4in)	○	H.H.A.
Iberis **Candytuft**	15cm x 5cm (6in x 2in)	○	H.A.

TUBS and BOXES

Impatiens **Busy Lizzy**	30cm x 25cm (12in x 10in)	●	H.H.A.
Impatiens balsamina **Camellia flowered balsam**	30cm x 12cm (12in x 5½in)	●	H.H.A.
Ipomoea tricolor **Morning glory**	3m x 10cm (10ft x 4in)	○	H.H.climber
Lathyrus odoratus **Sweet pea**	2m x 10cm (6½ft x 4in)	◑	H.H.climber
Lobelia trailing	30cm x 10cm (12in x 4in)	◑	H.H.A.
dwarf	15cm x 15cm (6in x 6in)	◑	H.H.A.
Matthiola **Stocks** mammoth	75cm x 30cm (30in x 12in)	●	H.A.
10-week dwarf	30cm x 10cm (12in x 4in)	●	H.A.
Molucella laevis **Bells of Ireland**	90cm x 40cm (3ft x 16in)	◑	H.A.
Myosotis **Forget-me-not**	25cm x 20cm (10in x 8in)	◑	H.A.
Nemesia	25cm x 10cm (10in x 4in)	○	H.H.A.
Nicotiana **Tobacco plant** dwarf mixtures	30cm x 10cm (12in x 4in)	●	H.A.
tall hybrids	70cm x 20cm (28in x 8in)	●	H.A.
Pelargonium	60cm x 40cm (24in x 16in)	○	T. sub-shrub
Petunia	25cm x 25cm (10in x 10in)	○	H.H.A.
Plumbago capensis	120cm x 50cm (4ft x 20in)	○	T.S.
Primula vulgaris **Polyanthus**	25cm x 20cm (10in x 8in)	◑	H.P.
Salpiglossis	45cm x 30cm (18in x 12in)	○	H.H.A.
Salvia horminum **Clary**	40cm x 10cm (16in x 4in)	○	H.A.
Salvia splendens	up to 40cm x 15cm (up to 16in x 6in)	○	H.H.A.
Schizanthus **Butterfly flower** giant strains	90cm x 40cm (3ft x 16in)	○	H.H.A.
dwarf strains	45cm x 20cm (18in x 8in)	○	H.H.A.
Solanum capsicastrum **Winter cherry**	30cm x 25cm (12in x 10in)	●	H.A.
Statice **Everlasting flower**	30cm x 10cm (12in x 4in)	○	H.A.
Tagetes **Marigold** jubilee hybrids	45cm x 30cm (18in x 12in)	○	H.H.A.
large flowered hybrids	90cm x 40cm (3ft x 16in)	○	H.H.A.
dwarf doubles and petites	20cm x 10cm (8in x 4in)	○	H.H.A.
Tropaeolum majus **Nasturtium** jewel mixed	25cm x 30cm (10in x 12in)	○	H.A.
Zinnia dwarf	15cm x 10cm (6in x 4in)	○	H.H.A.
large flowered hybrids	75cm x 30cm (30in x 12in)	○	H.H.A.

HOUSEPLANTS

It is probable that around 80 per cent of the houseplants sold through shops, florists and garden centres are purchased as gifts. It is therefore not uncommon for the recipient to be absolutely unaware of the plant's requirements unless it carries an explanatory label and often the gift is dead within a few weeks. However, with a little simple advice or help, an impulsive gesture can become an attractive and long-lasting addition to a household. For someone engaged in seriously building up a comprehensive collection of indoor plants there are many detailed publications which will give far more information than I have space for here, but there are certain plants which are seen everywhere and it seemed proper that, in a guide such as this, a representative selection should be described.

Many indoor plants are unaltered wild, tropical species which, because of their exotic foliage and lush habit, have been propagated and sold in temperate climates to decorate houses and offices. Such plants ask only a reasonable approximation of their natural jungle floor habitat in order to thrive; a well-lit site but no exposure to direct sunlight, moist soil at the root but not soggy or waterlogged, and a warm, moist atmosphere with no sharp, sudden variation in temperature. As a good general rule, flowering indoor plants such as azaleas, gardenias, *Saintpaulia* and *Streptocarpus* prefer a similar regime, but a hour or two's exposure to early morning or late afternoon sun does them no harm. There are, of course, one or two good old indestructables such as *Chlorophytum* (the spider plant), monstera (the Swiss cheese plant), helxine (babies' tears), sansevieria (mother-in-law's tongue) and *Rhoicissus* (grape ivy) which seem to survive under any conditions, but even these look a good deal more attractive if they are given a reasonable amount of attention. Wipe the dust off their leaves with a damp sponge now and then and give them a dose of fertilizer at regular intervals during the summer.

For hot, sunny, south-facing window sills the best choice is from the wide range of succulents offered by some retailers. These include such plants as *Crassula argentea* (the money plant or jade plant), pineapples, aechmeas and kalanchoës, as well as Mediterranean or South African natives such as pelargoniums, oleander (*Nerium oleander*) or the dwarf pomegranate (*Punica granatum* 'Nana').

HOUSEPLANTS

Aspidistra

Aspidistra

This handsome, broad-leafed foliage plant is remarkably tolerant and is happiest when left alone except for regular watering and dusting. It asks only for a well-lit position out of direct sunlight and a move into a slightly larger pot every four or five years. The flowers are a dusty purple colour and emerge at soil level, so they are frequently overlooked altogether. It is important that you do not use a chemical leaf shiner on aspidistras; if you do they will quickly die. It is sometimes possible to obtain a variegated form, but you must remove any plain green leaves or they will eventually take over and the variegation will disappear.

Azalea indica and Azalea japonica

A.indica

These dwarf, evergreen flowering shrubs thrive best in a relatively cool room and moist atmosphere. They should be well watered, but in hard-water districts the water must be boiled and cooled before use. A well-established plant of Azalea indica, repotted each year after flowering into fresh, lime-free compost and a slightly larger pot, will eventually attain a height of up to 80cm (2¾ft) and a spread of up to 100cm (3¼ft) while Azalea japonica (which is actually frost hardy) will attain a height of 130cm (4¼ft) and a spread of 60cm (2ft).

3–5

209

HOUSEPLANTS

Beloperone guttata

B.guttata

The **Shrimp Plant** derives its common name from the reddish-brown bracts which surround the slim, white, tubular flowers. The compost in the pot should be kept moist at all times but should not be allowed to become waterlogged. Regular feeding will keep the plant neat and compact and ensure plenty of flowers. Good light and normal room temperature are its other requirements. If potted on each autumn until it is in an 18cm (7in) pot, it will attain a height of about 90cm (36in) and a spread of up to 60cm (24in). Excessive heat or poor light will make the plant grow drawn and spindly.

🌸 4-10 ○

Chlorophytum

Chlorophytum

This is one of several unrelated plants which carry the common name **Spider Plant.** It is also known as **St Bernard's Lily** and **Dead Men's Fingers.** As a foliage plant it is one of the most indestructable species available. A well-grown plant will be 80cm (33in) across and 40cm (16in) tall, although in a hanging basket with its trailing stems bearing new plantlets it can often be up to 150cm (5ft) from top to bottom. The browning of the leaf-tips is usually a sign that it is being starved, but all you have to do is to pull the leaves off when they become unsightly, for there are always plenty of new ones to take their place. It will survive occasional periods of drought or waterlogging but should not be subjected too often to either.

🌸 1-12 ●

Clivia miniata

Clivia miniata

This striking flowering bulb with broad, strap-like leaves gives a display of bright orange flowers in early summer. Generally speaking, an older, more established plant gives the better show of flowers. The traditional method of cultivation is to keep the bulbs in their pot until they expand so much that they break it; then repot them into a slightly larger pot with fresh soil and a generous helping of composted manure or similar fertilizer. They prefer a well-lit position away from direct sunshine and will tolerate winter temperatures down to as low as 10°C (50°F) if they are kept dry. A mature specimen will be about 40cm (16in) tall when in flower and up to 60cm (24in) across.

 6

Dieffenbachia arvida 'Exotica'

D.arvida 'Exotica'

The **Dumb Cane** can attain a height of up to 200cm (6½ft) and a spread of 50cm (20in). It requires a shaded position, a moist atmosphere and a minimum temperature of 16°C (61°F). The compost should be moist at all times but must not become waterlogged, and the plant must be sheltered from any draughts. The sap in the leaves and stem is very poisonous and care should be taken if the plant is broken or injured. The individual leaves are not very long lived but many plants throw up new growth from the base to offset the bare appearance of the lower portion of older stems.

HOUSEPLANTS

Euphorbia pulcherrima

E.pulcherrima

The brilliant scarlet, white, cream or soft pink bracts surrounding the tiny flowers of the **Poinsettia** have made it a winter favourite. Sudden changes of temperature will severely injure the plant, so always buy from a warm, well-lit shop. After flowering it should be allowed to dry out completely for five or six weeks. Eventually, new growth will appear where the old leaves dropped off and then the plant can be watered and repotted into fresh John Innes No. 3. From September onwards they should have only natural daylight, as artificial light will inhibit the formation of the new flower buds and their surrounding bracts.

🌺 11-12 ○ ●●

Ficus benjamina and *Ficus elastica*

F.benjamina

The **Weeping Fig** and the **Rubber Plant** are dramatic foliage plants. *Ficus benjamina* can grow anything up to 4m (13ft) tall with a spread of 2m (6½ft) and requires a minimum temperature of 16°C (62°F). *Ficus elastica* prefers slightly cooler conditions (10°–15°C, 50°–62°F) and will attain a height of about 3m (10ft) and a spread of 1m (3¼ft) under ideal conditions. Both species detest being overwatered and should be planted in a free-draining compost. Wipe the dust from the broad leaves of the rubber plant, but put the weeping fig in the bath and use a mist sprayer once a month.

● ♦

HOUSEPLANTS

Ferns

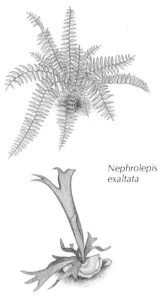

Nephrolepis exaltata

Platycerium bifurcatum

The most popular ferns are probably the **Maidenhair Fern** (*Adiantum raddianum*), the **Boston Fern** (*Nephrolepis exaltata*) and the **Stag's-horn Fern** (*Platycerium bifurcatum*). They all require similar conditions of warmth, shade and moisture although the maidenhair will tolerate lower temperatures than most ferns. They prefer, if possible, to be watered with rainwater or water that has been boiled and allowed to cool; the occasional spraying of the foliage with a mist of water from the same sources is beneficial. The broad fleshy fronds of the stag's-horn should not be wiped or handled. When well-established, any of these plants can be up to 60cm (24in) across and 40cm (16in) tall.

● ♦♦

Gardenia jasminoides

G. jasminoides

This superbly scented sub-tropical flowering shrub basically requires the same regime as azaleas, with moist, lime-free compost, even, warm temperatures and a well-lit position with little or no direct sunlight. The white, sweet-smelling blossoms are produced in May and June. Being a lime-hater it is best watered with rainwater or water that has been boiled and allowed to cool. **Gardenias** are fairly slow-growing, but with repotting every second year they can eventually reach over 100cm (3¼ ft) in height and 60cm (2ft) in width.

 5-6   ● ♦♦♦

HOUSEPLANTS

Gloxinia

Gloxinia

The richly coloured, velvety flowers of **Gloxinia** *(Sinningia speciosa)* appear in late summer, and the plant thrives on a light window sill provided that it does not get the full glare of the midday sun. The compost in the pot should be kept moist at all times but do not allow it to become waterlogged. After flowering, the plant can be stood outdoors in a sheltered corner while the leaves die down, and then the corm can be shaken out and repotted into a fresh helping of John Innes No. 2 compost, allowed to rest for a few weeks and then started into growth with modest watering. Usually the corms last two or three seasons, although some people keep them going for longer.

 7-9

Hibiscus rosa-sinensis

H.rosa-sinensis

Individual **Hibiscus** blooms are fairly short-lived, but with good light, regular feeding and plenty of water the plant will open a succession of blooms throughout the summer. The feeding and watering should be gradually reduced to nothing after the plant has finished flowering and it should be stood in a cool light place to rest for the winter. The foliage will dry up and drop but will appear again when you begin to water in February. If successfully potted on up to a 25cm (10in) pot, the plant will grow about 180cm (6ft) tall and 80cm (2¾ft) across. Repotting should be done in the spring.

 6-10

HOUSEPLANTS

Kalanchoë blossfeldiana

K.blossfeldiana

The normal flowering period for **Flaming Katy** is February to May, but one often sees it forced into flower for Christmas. Like many other succulents it likes a good light and will tolerate an hour or two of direct sunshine each day, as long as it is shielded from the midday glare. It takes up water fairly slowly, so care should be taken not to saturate the compost or the lower leaves will begin to rot. A well-established plant in a 15cm (6in) pot will be about 40cm (16in) tall in flower and up to 30cm (12in) across. It will do no harm to stand it in a shaded corner of the garden for the summer, provided it is not allowed to dry out.

 2-5

Maranta leuconeura

M. leuconeura
'Erythrophylla'

The exotic, fragile foliage of the **Prayer Plant** makes an attractive feature in a shaded position away from direct sunlight. It needs a moist atmosphere which can often be enhanced by standing the container on a tray of wet gravel or plunging the pot into a large container filled with moist peat or moss. It needs a weak liquid feed once a week during the summer and should be protected from drought and sudden temperature changes in winter. A well-established specimen will form a spreading dome about 60cm (24in) high and 40cm (16in) across. When potting on every other year use a light, free-draining compost such as John Innes No. 2.

HOUSEPLANTS

Peperomia caperata

P.caperata

This handsome compact little plant is often used in bottle gardens. The dark green corrugated leaves form an attractive mound seldom more than 30cm (12in) across and 20cm (8in) high. The plant produces pale spikes of flowers in summer but these are not particularly striking.

Peperomias need moderate warmth and good light but no direct sunlight. They like a moist atmosphere and grow well in a container planted up with several kinds of plants. The variegated form needs maximum north light and is rather more susceptible to damage by overwatering or sudden changes in temperature.

 6-8

Saintpaulia ionantha

'Diana Pink'

'Diana Blue'

African Violets have a reputation for being difficult to care for, but most people seem to manage. They like good light and will even tolerate early morning or late afternoon sun but not summer's midday glare. Their compost should be kept moist but not waterlogged and they will seldom withstand temperatures lower than 13°C. Aphid attacks are best dealt with by a systemic insecticide — there is one on the market in the form of a cardboard 'pin' which you simply push into the soil so that the insecticide is taken up through the plant's roots. Regular feeding will keep the plant flowering for most of the year.

 1-12

Scindapsus

Scindapsus

In a moist, well-lit position out of direct sunlight, the **Devil's Ivy** will make a striking foliage plant. It can either be allowed to trail down from a pot hung high on a wall or bookshelf or trained to climb up a moss-covered pole (the latter is better since the damp moss helps to maintain the moist atmosphere that the plant favours). Generally, conditions in the average household mean that the plant will grow slowly and it should require repotting only every two or three years. A five-year-old plant in a 15cm (6in) pot could be as large as 150cm (5ft) from top to bottom and about 40cm (16in) wide in ideal conditions.

Streptocarpus × hybridus

S. × hybridus

The **Cape Primrose** is a popular spring- and summer-flowering plant. Its very long, oval leaves give it a somewhat ungainly appearance when not in flower, but when you see it crowned with a multitude of sprays of delicately marked pastel-coloured flowers it is easy to understand its appeal. It enjoys very similar treatment to *Saintpaulia* with good light, a warm, moist atmosphere and regular watering during the growing period — add liquid feed before and during flowering. The watering can be reduced during the autumn and winter and the feeding left off altogether. Large clumps can be divided in spring and repotted into John Innes No. 2.

 4-7

HOUSEPLANTS

Tradescantia fluminensis and *Zebrina pendula*

Tradescantia fluminensis

Zebrina pendula

These trailing plants are similar in many respects. They tolerate sun or shade and will produce a wealth of foliage spreading everywhere during the summer. When you see the shoots twining through and wrapping round everything near them you can easily see how they got their nickname of **Wandering Sailor.** To keep them in good condition they must be well fed and well watered. It is often necessary to cut them back to within one or two leaf joints from the base in spring to keep the plants tidy and remove the build-up of dead foliage that has been collecting through the winter.

 7-10

Yucca

Yucca

This curious plant tolerates drier conditions than many other houseplants and requires little in the way of care or feeding. Usually it remains at the height at which you buy it, although the foliage crown or side shoots gradually expand. It prefers good light without direct sunlight and regular, careful watering. In winter, in a centrally-heated atmosphere, it will benefit from being stood on a tray of wet gravel or being plunged into a larger container filled with wet peat or moss. However, care should be taken that the compost in the pot itself does not become too wet.

Botanical Nomenclature

In selecting plants it is useful to understand the differences between the various botanical terms such as *species, cultivar, hybrid* and so on, which are used in this book.

SPECIES The basic unit of reference upon which plant classification is based. Essentially, a group of morphologically very similar and interfertile individuals, which show constant differences from allied groups

Groups of allied species are classified together in units called *Genera* (singular: *Genus*) and genera are grouped in *Families*. There are further levels in this hierarchical classification, but these three are those which most concern the gardener. The concept of 'genus' is widely confused with that of 'family'.

As more and more species are grouped together the number and nature of the characters which define the resultant group will change. At the species level all individuals will look very similar, differing only in a few minor features. The members of a genus will often share a general plan but will show variations on that theme, whereas families will often be defined by more detailed characters which do not necessarily dictate the overall appearance of the plants; these often concern the basic structure of the flowers and fruits.

VARIETIES and FORMS Terms to be used with care since they have a formal botanical meaning as well as a much looser usage in everyday speech. Botanically they are the *varietas* (var.) and *forma* (f.), infraspecific categories to describe variation encompassed by the species. A var. will usually be defined by a number of characters and may exist in local populations, a f. will usually represent a plant differing from the normal by a single character and usually appears as one or few scattered individuals in a larger population of the normal plant.

CULTIVARS This is a term used for groups of plants which it is useful to distinguish for horticultural purposes. A cultivar may be selected from wild populations of a species (or hybrid) or may be selected from species or hybrids in cultivation. In other words, not all cultivars are hybrids, not all hybrids (whatever their origin) are cultivars. Cultivars may be defined by one or more characters (and can cover the same variation recognized botanically are var. or f.). It is most often used for *clone* (i.e. a collection of individuals all ultimately derived by vegetative means from a single original plant) but this is not necessarily always true or necessary.

HYBRIDS Theoretically the offspring of the cross between any two individuals, but most widely applied to the progeny of an interspecific cross. Hybrids, will often show a greatly extended range of variation compared with the parents, and individual selections from this range may be described as cultivars.

SPORTS A shoot differing from the rest of the plant in one or more characters which are not normally exhibited by the parent (variegation, flower colour, leaf form, etc.). If removed and grown on, a complete plant can be obtained showing the abnormal characteristics. Once propagated it may be given a cultivar name.

INDEX

List of Common and Botanical names. Illustrations of a plant are not indicated unless separated from the text. For these, the page number is in italics.

INDEX

221

INDEX

INDEX

INDEX